Prestel Mus

CH00675174

Hamburger Bahnhof
Museum for the Present — Berlin

Prestel

Munich · New York

© Prestel-Verlag
Munich · New York, 1997

© of works illustrated: see p. 144

© of floor plans on front inside cover:
PERFORM, Berlin

Photos: Jörg P. Anders, Lutz Deppe,
Reinhard Friedrich, Raimund Kummer,
Jochen Littkemann, Helge Mundt,
Gerhard Murza, Galerie Barbara Weiss,
Werner Zellien, Jens Ziehe (all Berlin),
Giorgio Massa (Florence), Archiv Bern-
hard Leitner (Vienna), Lothar Schnepf,
Simon Vogel (Cologne), Happening-
Archiv Vostell (Malpartida), Hayward
Gallery (London), Westfälisches Landes-
museum für Kunst- und Kulturgeschichte
(Münster)

Editors: Britta Schmitz and Dieter Scholz
assisted by Silke Giersch, Karola
Kostede, Immo Wagner-Douglas

Prestel-Verlag
Mandlstrasse 26, 80802 Munich,
Germany
Tel.: (+49–89) 38 17 09–0;
Fax: (+49–89) 38 17 09–35
and 16 West 22nd Street,
New York, NY 10010, USA
Tel.: (212) 627–8199;
Fax: (212) 627–9866

Prestel books are available worldwide.
Please contact your nearest bookseller
or write to either of the above
addresses for information concerning
your local distributor.

For CIP data, please see page 144.

Translated from the German
by Penelope Crowe
Edited by Jacqueline Guigui-Stolberg
Designed by Maja Thorn, Berlin
Lithography by Reprographia, Lahr
Typeset by Mega-Satz-Service, Berlin
Printed and bound by
Passavia Druckerei GmbH, Hutthurm

Printed in Germany
ISBN 3-7913-1731-8 (English edition)
ISBN 3-7913-1713-X (German edition)

Printed on acid-free paper

**Hamburger Bahnhof
Museum For the Present
State Museums of Berlin —
Stiftung Preussischer Kulturbesitz**
Invalidenstrasse 50/51
10557 Berlin
Tel.: (+49–30) 39 78 34–0
Fax: (+49–30) 39 78 34–13

Opening Hours
Daily except Mondays
9 a.m. – 5 p.m.
Saturdays and Sundays
10 a.m. – 5 p.m.

**Museum Education Department and
Visitor Service**
For information on guided group tours,
call:
Tel.: (+49–30) 830 14 66 / 20 35 54 44

Public Tours
Every other Sunday at 11 a.m.

Restaurant
Open daily except Mondays
9 a.m. – 5 p.m.

Members of the Hamburger Bahnhof's
supporters' association enjoy numerous
benefits. For information, contact:

**Verein der
Freunde der Nationalgalerie**
Rankestrasse 21
10789 Berlin
Tel.: (+49–30) 2 14 96 187
Fax: (+49–30) 2 14 96 100

Front cover: Joseph Beuys, *Richtkräfte*,
1974–77 (detail); see p. 20
Back cover: View of the eastern Ehren-
hoff wing, August 1996
Pages 4–5:
The Hamburger Bahnhof —
Museum for the Present, Berlin.
Entrance from Invalidenstrasse,
August 1996
Pages 12–13:
View of the newly restored historical
hall, August 1996
Pages 16–17:
View of the newly built East Gallery
designed by Josef Paul Kleihues, 1996
Pages 142–43:
Günther Uecker, *Westtor — vernagelt*
(Western Gate — Nailed Up), 1996,
13 1/2 x 10 1/4 x 2 ft.

Contents

Foreword

The Hamburger Bahnhof
Museum for the Present — Berlin and
the State Museums of Berlin

On November 30, 1987, the advisory board of the Stiftung Preussischer Kulturbesitz (Foundation for Prussian Cultural Heritage) met and considered for the first time the proposal put forward by the state of Berlin to use the so-called Hamburger Bahnhof (Hamburg Train Station), the former Museum of Transportation and Building, for the presentation of contemporary art. At this meeting the senator responsible for cultural affairs, Volker Hassemer, and the senator for finances, Günter Rexrodt, declared Berlin's readiness to extend and refurbish the Hamburger Bahnhof as a museum of contemporary art at the expense of the state. The state would allow the Stiftung Preussischer Kulturbesitz to use the building rent-free and furthermore agreed to pay part of the museum's running expenses.

For the state museums, this generous offer has proven to be the ideal solution to their problems — problems that were growing literally day by day — involving the display of contemporary art. The Neue Nationalgalerie (New National Gallery) could not provide nearly enough space and, then as now, was continually being rearranged to make room for temporary exhibitions. Beyond this, it was in Berlin's interest to concentrate all efforts on keeping its private collections in the city. This was particularly true in the case of Dr. Erich Marx, with whom concrete agreements were made in order to ward off other offers for his collection. Only the Hamburger Bahnhof, which came under Senate administration in 1984, and which had since been renovated and used for temporary exhibitions, could provide adequate space. The senator for finances then sought an occupant who would be prepared to assume the greater part of the running expenses, in particular those for staff. Even then — before the Wall came down — money

was tight and the willingness of the federal government to give additional funding to Berlin was limited.

It is, however, important to note that despite the most difficult circumstances, the founding of the Museum for the Present in the Hamburger Bahnhof was never questioned by the Senate or House of Representatives. This is cause for gratitude.

This unique building complex, with rooms divided into relatively small areas in the three-storied entrance structure, the long halls in the wings flanking the Great Court, the three-aisled hall of the Museum of Transportation, and the newly constructed main hall with its high vaulted ceiling, was thought to be an ideal space to bring together works from the contemporary art collections of four museums. Drawings and prints from the Kupferstichkabinett (Print Collection) are seen alongside objects from the collection of the Nationalgalerie. Examples of design and handcrafts have been contributed by the Kunstgewerbemuseum (Museum of Applied Art), and architectural materials, photographs, posters, and applied graphics from the Kunstbibliothek (Art Library) are shown. The most varied ways of presenting objects in different combinations are therefore possible. These possibilities are used alternately, allowing for some areas to be permanent and others to be semi-permanent. At the same time, it is necessary to carefully preserve the character of the museum itself. Before us lies an exciting and productive period during which the general director will observe with great interest how four museums cooperate with one another while considering themselves independent. The experience gained from this collaboration will be of use to the Museumsinsel and the museum complex Dahlem, where cooperation is the key to solving the tasks that lie ahead.

For the Hamburger Bahnhof, the problem exists as to how to remain a museum for the present when some works of art no longer belong to this period and would be better exhibited in

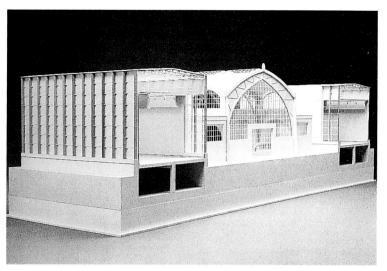

Model of the Hamburger Bahnhof — Museum for the Present, Berlin, by Josef Paul Kleihues, 1989

another place, within their proper historical contexts. For some time to come this exhibition possibility will be provided by the Neue Nationalgalerie. But even now we have to consider that the Hamburger Bahnhof must have its second new wing completed in the near future, and that the extension to the Neue Nationalgalerie, conceived in 1987, will also be built to house the art of the 20th century in a historical context.

When we started with the Hamburger Bahnhof project, we looked out at the barred windows beyond the shipping canal and were much concerned about the border control barracks directly in front of the entrance. To some people, the location of the planned museum seemed too out-of-the-way. That feeling has passed, and within a few years this place will be among the liveliest in Berlin. To be part of a living Berlin and to create space for contemporary art is the mission of the Hamburger Bahnhof.

Wolf-Dieter Dube
General Director of the
State Museums of Berlin

The Hamburger Bahnhof as Museum for the Present in Berlin

The Hamburger Bahnhof, opened on November 1st, 1996 is quite intentionally not called "Museum for Contemporary Art," but far more appropriately "Museum for the Present." This term is more comprehensive and acknowledges the role of the new museum not only in many in presenting fine art but aspects of modern life: artists, media, everyday culture, discussions, music, performances, and readings. The present does not just encompass objects made by artists; the term "present" also conditions the way in which we view objects today.

It thus would make no sense to judge the relevance of this house to contemporary life by examining *when* exactly individual works were produced. It is of far greater importance to follow the continually changing and transforming image of this house through steps in time, which, in conjunction with its daily events, produces new and completely differing focuses time and time again. This museum for the present is not static, as its lay-out allows for alterations in the positioning of individual works or groups of work. This flexibility in being able to frequently change exhibits is not merely necessary in order to display the steadily increasing collection, which far exceeds the capacity of all wall and floor space, but also concerns the conservation demanded by, for example, works on paper. The Hamburger Bahnhof will become the museum of the 21st century — so longed for — not only because of its exhibited works but also because of its approach to its task and its ability to reinvent itself. It is unimportant what sorts of utopias are developed in Berlin; it must always be remembered that this new house in its present form could only be realized because the state of Berlin, which owns the building, offered exhibition space for objects in private collections, particularly the Marx Collection.

There are very few collections in Europe that possess the same denseness of quality, and Erich Marx is a collector who thinks on a museum-like scale. Put together over the last twenty years, this collection's exceptional value is due to Marx's decision at the outset to restrict it to a few artists and to concentrate on larger, interdependent work cycles completed over the years. This aim developed from the realization that an artist's consistency of thought on painting or sculpture and its visual expression is more clearly demonstrated by a number of works than by a single example.

The main building of the Hamburger Bahnhof, lithograph, c. 1852

View of the main station hall, c. 1908

The four major artists of the Marx Collection are Joseph Beuys, Robert Rauschenberg, Cy Twombly, and Andy Warhol. Their work, artistic concepts, and approach have had differing but a decisive influence on artistic, art-historical, and aesthetic debate. Like leitmotifs, Joseph Beuys and Andy Warhol will appear in different media in various parts of the museum. Works by Cy Twombly and Robert Rauschenberg will find a long-term home in the spacious East Gallery alongside the pictures of Andy Warhol and those of Roy Lichtenstein, whose pictures were acquired at a later date.

Besides maintaining this collection's links with Berlin, the state museums also felt the need to display the stocks of 20th century art, hidden in their different departments, to better advantage. The coupling of both ideas led, at first, to a new concept for the use of the Hamburger Bahnhof: not as just another museum, but as a new forum for communication between private and public collections in a dynamic environment.

Despite this resolve, it soon became evident that the Hamburger Bahnhof in its present, still incomplete form (the construction of a second wing for a picture gallery could not as yet be undertaken), would be too small to exhibit the Marx Collection in its entirety.

The basic concept, not to found a new museum, but to make a revitalized and ever-changing exhibition space inside a historic building, has been adhered to up to this day. Along with the Marx Collection, the other sources of works for this lively forum are the permanent collections of the Nationalgalerie, the Kupferstichkabinett, the Kunstbibliothek, and the Kunstgewerbemuseum. The Hamburger Bahnhof does not only represent a cross-fertilization involving different collections, but includes all the different media employed by artists. These are not only shown in separate rooms, but will also be found together in the halls used for events. This (for Berlin) new and unique concept required that the historic building of the Hamburger Bahnhof be converted and extended by Josef Paul Kleihues, who also took into account the need for a certain logical sequence of rooms, as in a museum.

The eventful history of the Hamburger Bahnhof began 150 years ago when it was the terminal of the Ham-

Passage to the East Wing, 1983

burg–Berlin railroad line. The first journey of 178 miles from Berlin to Hamburg took place on December 12, 1846 and lasted a good eight hours. The three-storied main station hall was constructed in a late classical style in 1846–47 to the plans of the architect and railway pioneer Friedrich Neuhaus (1797–1876). In order to be turned around, the locomotives were driven through two high round arched gates onto a turntable in front of the building.

The imposing station hall served as a model for all of Berlin's large terminal stations in the second half of the 19th century, but is now the only one of its kind which still exists.

As a result of the enormous increase in passenger and freight rail traffic in the second half of the last century, and despite various extensions, the station was soon unable to fulfill its function. It had to be closed in 1884 and its role was taken over by the much larger

View of the West Wing during renovation, 1994

Renovation of windows in the main hall, May 1996

Lehrter Bahnhof, which had been built thirteen years previously.

After the platforms and tracks had been demolished, the main station hall was converted for residential and administrative use in 1885–86. This was to be its destiny for the next two decades.

Long-cherished plans to erect a transportation museum in Berlin led to the decision, in 1904, to remodel the Hamburger Bahnhof as a transportation and building museum. The required conversions, which took two years to complete, left its external appearance virtually unchanged; the ground floor was, however, altered considerably. The original open platform between the two side wings was replaced by a 95 x 233-feet great iron hall flanked by an aisle on each side, built to plans by Ernst Schwartz. This still forms the center of the museum today.

The museum was extremely popular and had to be extended frequently. In

Renovation of windows near the entrance of the main hall, May 1996

the years 1910–11 and 1914–16, the main station hall was enlarged by the addition of two wings built at right angles to the facade on either side of the Great Court.

In this form the museum remained unchanged until the outbreak of World War II. During the air-raids on Berlin in 1943, the building was severely damaged more than once and had to be closed down completely.

In the confusion following the war, the Hamburger Bahnhof was mistakenly put under the jurisdiction of the Reichsbahndirektion (Ost) (Imperial Railway, east). The fact that no train had left the station since 1884 and that the building had served as a transportation and building museum since 1906 was overlooked. In the context of the negotiations in 1983 on the administration of the S-Bahn (the suburban train network), the Berlin Senate and the Reichsbahn (the East German railway) agreed that the museum and its contents should be handed over to the administration of the Berlin Senate from February 1st, 1984.

The Hamburger Bahnhof was partially restored for the 750th anniversary celebrations for the city of Berlin in 1987. This work was carried out by the architect Winnetou Kampmann before the future function of the building was defined. It was reopened as an exhibition space in 1987 for the exhibition "Reise nach Berlin" (Journey to Berlin).

An important example was given by Harald Szeemann in 1988 with his exhibition "Zeitlos" (Timeless), demonstrating how the building could be used as a showplace for present-day art. In the same year, an agreement to devote a museum to contemporary art was reached between the Senate and the Stiftung Preussischer Kulturbesitz.

The architect Josef Paul Kleihues was commissioned to undertake the comprehensive reconstruction work and the building of two new side wings. For many reasons, these plans could not be fully realized, and the work could only be carried out after long delays. As yet, only the East Gallery has been completed. A further DM 25 million is required for the planned construction of the

Passage to the East Wing after renovation, August 1996

Andy Warhol, Portrait of Erich Marx, *1978,*
Silk screen, acrylic on canvas,
40 x 40 in.; The Marx Collection

West Gallery. The new dimension gained by Berlin through the Hamburger Bahnhof is not only brought about by the exceptional Marx Collection, but also lies in the fact that a new, dynamic presentation form combining several institutions and initiatives has been created. A unique space, both in conception and structure, has emerged. With its ever-changing character and projects continually exploring present-day questions, it is more than able to stand up to the tests of European and international objectives. It is possible that the Hamburger Bahnhof will not be able to provide an answer for many of these questions. It will, however, itself ask questions through its ever freshly-acquired material: questions arising from problems of our time.

Dieter Honisch
Director of the Nationalgalerie

The Works in the Hamburger Bahnhof Museum for the Present — Berlin

Contributors:

Eugen Blume	E.B.	Maria Martinez	M.M.
Alexander Dückers	A.D.	Britta Schmitz	B.S.
Dieter Honisch	D.H.	Angela Schneider	A.S.
Karola Kostede	K.K.	Dieter Scholz	D.S.
Jörg Makarinus	J.M.	Peter-Klaus Schuster	P.K.S.
Lutz Malke	L.M.	Immo Wagner-Douglas	I.W.D.
		Friedegund Weidemann	F.W.

Joseph Beuys 1921–86

Richtkräfte (Directional Forces)
1974–77

100 wooden blackboards, 3 easels,
1 walking stick, 1 light box with
photograph   7 1/2 x 39 x 17 ft.

Nationalgalerie, acquired 1976 with funding from
the state of Berlin

Some of the most important ways in
which the "extended thought processes" of Joseph Beuys were demonstrated were in public speaking,
lecturing, and conversation. From
the 1960s until his death, this "constant conference" helped Beuys to
develop "a better form of thinking,
feeling, and wanting" (J. Beuys).
Eloquent testimony of this "talking
work" may be found in numerous
board drawings such as in installa-
tions like Das Kapital or Richtkräfte,
which are like imaginary archives but
which, as in the blackboards of the
Marx Collection, also "speak" individually. The board drawings are not
the secondary aids of some past dis-

cussion but are, on the contrary, independent drawings. Although they
include the written word, they go
beyond it.

The formation of terms is unthink-
able without an imagination that ex-
plores areas unable to be expressed
in language, thus demanding again
and again the creation of new terms.
The board drawings suggest this area.
Its depth is defined in drawing and its
surface in its abstraction. Richtkräfte
was created in conjunction with an
exhibition at the Institute of Contemporary Arts (ICA) in London, during
which Beuys organized seminars on
his artistic theories. With the help of
diagrams and drawings on school
blackboards, he outlined the funda-
mentals of a society transformed by
an extended definition of art. Once
he had written and drawn on the
boards, he threw them to the floor.
Later, these one 100 blackboards
were laid on a wooden platform and
three of them were put on easels.
This archive of Beuys' visions, which

like a motto for his art, the words: "make the secrets productive." The three boards on the easels signal the "educational task" that Beuys wanted to link up to different intellectual standpoints. The board on the left bears only the two mutated vowels "ö-ö": an articulation seemingly related to and yet more suggestive than the phonetic poems written by the Dadaists. Beuys is interested in language as a formative process, in the production of sound by use of speech organs and linguistic genius. The "ö-ö sounds" take us back to the beginnings of mankind and the corresponding development of language from animal articulation to the spoken word.

The walking stick hanging in front of the board with its curved end downwards was used in this way by Beuys during the London exhibition to demonstrate the energy connecting spirit and matter. The direction of movement leads downwards into the earth and, by following the curve and moving upwards, attains the intellectual domain. It was for Beuys, who is this case was referring to Rudolf Steiner, a matter of extraordinary importance to combine thought with the experiences of the senses.

On the illuminated opaque glass of the black box at the back right, we can make out the figure of a hare. The shape of this hare had been formed quite accidentally on the rubber stopper of the walking stick and

seems to drift as if on a raft, has been removed from the didactic approach to a sculptural form that places the secret above factual knowledge. One of the blackboards on an easel bears,

Joseph Beuys   1921–86

Blackboard from *Richtkräfte*   1974
Wooden board, blackboard paint, chalk, fixative   35 $^1/_2$ x 47 $^3/_4$ in.
Nationalgalerie, acquired 1976

was later enlarged and integrated by Beuys into the *Richtkräfte* environment. Animal forms occupy a central role in Joseph Beuys' work. In particular the hare, with its powers of incarnation, was considered by Beuys to be an exemplary creature, and it appears in many of his works. In his happening "Wie man dem toten Hasen die Bilder

Joseph Beuys 1921–86

——— ? 1952

Drawing from "The Secret Block for a Secret Person in Ireland"

Iron chloride, chamois-colored drawing card 29 $^{1}/_{2}$ x 19 $^{3}/_{4}$ in.

The Marx Collection

erklärt" (How to Explain Pictures to a Dead Hare), he elucidated his drawing to a hare. For Beuys, drawing was an elemental procedure with which he endeavored to probe the quintessential forces of nature. It is an important aspect of Beuys' work, opening a window onto a world beyond rational thought processes.

It was in 1974 that Beuys first put together a larger group of drawings for an exhibition at the Museum of Modern Art in Oxford under the title "The Secret Block for a Secret Person in Ireland." The exhibition subsequently moved to several other English museums. By the time the Kunstmuseum (Museum of Art) in Basel

exhibited the cycle in 1977, Beuys had extended it with a further 64 sheets. For the large exhibition at the Guggenheim Museum in New York he had expanded it yet again by another 23 drawings. The final volume of this block of graphic work totaled 456 sheets with widely differing formats using the most varied media and techniques of drawing. The drawings were shown for the first time in Germany in the 1982 exhibition of the Marx Collection at the Nationalgalerie, Berlin. Again and again, Beuys specially selected drawings from his extensive production of graphic work for inclusion in the secret block. The 456 drawings selected for the collection "Secret Block for a Secret Person in Ireland" form a work whose subtlety challenges the senses, inviting the viewer into the artist's imagination and letting him share in thought processes which Beuys developed over many years. The cycle begins with early works from the 1940s and ends in 1976. The consistently high quality of drawing is extraordinary. It was achieved from the outset, apparently without any youthful insecurity or need for preparatory sketches, and continued until Beuys' death. Everything Beuys formulated verbally was inspired by his drawings. His holistic concepts of society are born from the energy fields explored in his drawings. Beuys tried out vastly differing materials in an effort to express this particular intellectual or spiritual sphere. The range of graphic expression extends from drawings in pencil to water and oil painting to unusual paint substances such as iron chloride, bronze gold, blood, iodine, and many others. The paper itself is frequently collaged, emphasizing its plastic dimension. Drawings are cut up and joined together again in new ways with bits of felt and cardboard added. The figures range from the shapes of humans and animals, to geological formations and abstract forms. They represent a field of exploration, a graphic laboratory which does not look for its meaning in naturalistic illustration but seeks invisible powers beyond the reach of rational scientific methods of discovery. The drawings do not address the interpreter who attempts to decipher them on a rational level; they speak to other fields of energy. As an entirety, they describe an intellectual space, imbued with secrets, that has no equivalent in language. To delineate individual topoi is to give the mere outlines, and thus ignore what is fundamental. It is only later that Joseph Beuys' ideas, dedicated to redesigning society as the artistic process of creation, detach themselves from these graphic fields of energy. It was only the drawings that, as he himself said, made him capable of developing such a holistic vision. Beuys considered this "secret block" to be an open field of experimentation upon whose creative energy he could draw. He recognized in its erratic dimension a sort of intellectual power station.

The iron sculpture *Doppelfond* of 1954 is based on the shape of a cross created by Beuys in around 1953 and executed in basalt as a gravestone wich was commissioned by the Düsseldorf collector Joseph Koch in 1955–56. On the gravestone, the same iron mould, which is cast twice in *Doppelfond*, forms the horizontal bar of the cross. The form, which

Joseph Beuys   1921–86

——— ?   1953

Montage from "The Secret Block for a Secret Person in Ireland"

watercolors, bronze gold, crayon, ink, pencil, different papers.
24 3/4 x 19 3/4 in.

The Marx Collection

rises steeply from the floor and looks like a mountain ridge with a central plateau, is an abstraction of the head and arms of Jesus Christ. The doubled crossbeam suggests the descent from the cross and the burial of the body. In *Doppelfond*, the cross as symbol is imagined as a directional force but not given a clearly defined form. The lightning conductor, complete with a grounding panel, which is attached to the lower end of one of the iron forms, seems to refer to the storm which, like divine energy, vented itself over Golgotha at the moment of Christ's death on the cross. Golgotha is for Beuys the end and a new beginning in one.

Joseph Beuys' Media Archive

No other artist had such a presence in the media. Beuys' unusually wide-reaching political involvement attracted public interest early on. Many of his spectacular appearances, happenings, speeches, and interviews have been recorded on film or tape. For the first time, the attempt is being made in the Hamburger Bahnhof to bring together all filmed and taped material in one place and make it accessible to the public. Using computers it is now possible for visitors to choose from ten hours of archive material which is accessible under various keywords. Complete films can also be viewed. Among these are *Eurasienstab* from 1968, *Coyote I, I Like America and America Likes Me* from

Joseph Beuys   1921–86

Doppelfond   1954

Iron, copper, zinc, steel, aluminum, brass   14 $^{3}/_{4}$ x 4 $^{1}/_{2}$ x 9 $^{1}/_{2}$ ft.

The Marx Collection

Joseph Beuys 1921–86

Coyote III
Concert
Tokyo June 2, 1984

Videoprint
Nationalgalerie, Joseph Beuys Media
Archive

1974, *Coyote III* from 1984, *Beuys und seine Klasse* (Beuys and His Class) by Hans Emmerling, and *Jeder Mensch ein Künstler* (Every Person an Artist) by Werner Krüger as well as several group discussions. The films and numerous taped talks and interviews give insight into the social, political, and artistic concept Beuys summed up in the term "soziale Plastik." Beuys per-

ceived speech as a plastic process which does not merely mean the articulation of sound using the speech organs, but certainly also includes the forming of sentences and above all one's reaction to the language of others. Beuys demonstrated this several times during his 100-day-long "permanenten Konferenz" at the documenta in Kassel.

The work *Unschlitt/Tallow* ("Unschlitt" comes from the old High German for tallow) shows Beuys' plastic theory in its social as well as its aesthetic dimension. This uncompromising sculpture was made for the "Skulptur" exhibition of 1977 in Münster. Suggesting the ubiquitous use of concrete and the destruction of urban structure in most German towns, Beuys recreated the empty, dead space of a ramp above a pedestrian tunnel in Münster. The creation of this sculpture, "which does not get cold" (J.Beuys) was like a healing process, the reviving through warmth of a "cold place." Beuys had transformed the interior form of a useless, dead space, and had elevated it — or, it could be said, saved it.

In 1976, in the central space of the German pavilion of the Venice Biennale, Beuys erected his memorial monument *Strassenbahnhaltestelle* (A Monument to the Future). This memorial, cast in iron, represented an environment which extended far beyond its biographical significance.

Joseph Beuys 1921–86

Unschlitt / Tallow 1977

Tallow fat, plaster, thermo-elements,
transformer, steel, gauges
31 $^{1}/_{4}$ x 10 x 6 $^{1}/_{2}$ ft.

The Marx Collection, owned by the state of Berlin

26 Joseph Beuys

The recollection of that tram stop
Zum Eisernen Mann ("at the iron
man") at the end of Nassauer Allee in
Kleve, where the six-year-old Beuys
often used to wait on his way to
school, takes us back to the culture

of his home on the Lower Rhine. Without realizing the significance of those strange iron parts which stuck out between the tracks and the road, the child intuitively perceived that place, where the remains of one of the memorials built by the 17th-century prince and enlightened philosopher Johann Moritz von Nassau-Siegen were linked to a modern method of transportation. In the original version, the barrel of a canon

additional shining section of track whose curve suggested the earth's orbit as well as the infinity and speed of thought.

In the second version of *Strassenbahnhaltestelle* from 1979, the tracks have a dull and rusty finish, the streetcar line is no longer in use, the column and kegs have been joined to recall an archaic vehicle and have been put aside. The tracks fork, showing paths in two possible directions. Beuys saw the catastrophe mankind is heading towards at the end of this century and made an attempt to develop a means of deliverance.

Das Ende des 20. Jahrhunderts, a work consisting of several parts,

Joseph Beuys   1921–86

Strassenbahnhaltestelle
(A Monument to the Future)
2nd version   1979
29 pieces of iron   27 $\frac{1}{2}$ x 8 x 2 $\frac{1}{4}$ ft.
The Marx Collection

decorated with a dragon's mouth, a so-called "Feldschlange" (fieldsnake) was surrounded by four powder kegs. Beuys had a cast made of this and rearranged the parts as a momument in Venice. The emotional world of the child, in which the pacifist symbol was experienced as a natural form, is recalled and further developed in the new arrangement and, through the image of the monument, linked to the act of thinking. The motif of the male head protruding out of the barrel of the cannon is like the illustration of a path of experience beyond our powers of comprehension. Christ's Passion, death, and resurrection seem to overlap in this unusual crucifixion, to occur simultaneously. It is the resurrection of God incarnate out of materialism — as Beuys himself formulated it.

In Venice, the vertically placed Passion column was fitted with an

opens our century in both directions: far back into prehistoric times as well as into a future as yet unknown. As geological objects, the basalt steles have traversed an inconceivable space of time. Their origins date back to a time when the earth in its present form was created and the first organic life appeared. But it was man who was first able to break the stones out of a context lasting millions of years and to expose them to creative shaping, contemplation, and even destruction. Propped up on pallets, wooden sticks and a jack, the basalt steles bear witness to this interference in nature. Whatever form this hazardous undertaking which culminates in the 20th century takes depends solely on the conduct of mankind.

E.B.

Joseph Beuys 1921–86

Das Ende des 20. Jahrhunderts
(The End of the 20th Century)
1982–83

21 basalt stones, felt, clay, stone-lifter, crowbar
Measurements vary according to construction

The Marx Collection, owned by the state of Berlin

Robert Rauschenberg   born 1925
lives in Captiva, Florida

Untitled   1951–52
Oil, collage on canvas
6 $^1/_2$ x 4 $^3/_4$ ft.
The Marx Collection

Robert Rauschenberg played a very important role in the development of Pop Art. His two early works, *Untitled* and *Pink Door,* have similarities in their visual structure but are totally different in their materials.

The first work dates back to Rauschenberg's student days at Black Mountain College in North Carolina, where he attended the class of Josef Albers, who had emigrated from Germany in 1933. The painting style of the former Bauhaus teacher was remarkable for its high degree of rationality and precision. A different, expressive use of color was introduced to Rauschenberg by Robert Motherwell, another lecturer at Black Mountain College, who belonged to a section of the Abstract Expressionist movement. With its bold brushstrokes, the right side of Rauschen-

berg's two-part picture refers to this style which at that time dominated the art world. In contrast to this, the left side has an even, monochromatic layer of paint reminiscent of the severity and solid blocks of color in Albers' art. Here, Rauschenberg presents the differing alternatives in painting, setting them together in the picture as equals.

The series "Black Paintings," to which *Untitled* belongs, pre-dates the "White Paintings" in which the artistic element was reduced to a minimum. Following on from this, the series of "Red Paintings" culminated in the work *Pink Door.* Again, a vertical structure divided into two halves forms the basis of this work. Paint applied vigorously over collaged fabric elements of the left-hand side faces a calm right-hand side with gauze stretched tautly between horizontal wooden boards. Two hinges reveal that the parts are movable. After *Pink Door* followed space-grasping objects which Rauschenberg called "Combines." These free-standing constructions were covered with newspaper cuttings, photographs, and assorted objects, while some areas were painted. *Pink Door,* although still referring to the wall surface, can be seen as the first "Combine" painting.

After the "Combines," Rauschenberg returned to two-dimensional types of painting which are often

Robert Rauschenberg   born 1925
lives in Captiva, Florida

Pink Door 1954
Oil, collage on cotton, door frame, gauze, door
7 $^1/_2$ x 4 ft.
The Marx Collection

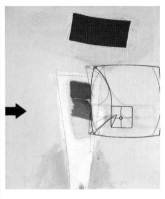

Robert Rauschenberg   born 1925
lives in Captiva, Florida

Stripper   1962
Oil, wood, fabric, sheet iron, wire,
printed paper on canvas
2 parts: 8 x 3 ¹/₂ ft. (left),
4 x 3 ¹/₂ ft. (right)
The Marx Collection

grounded in diverse origins. Having
previously worked with John Cage at
Black Mountain College, Rauschenberg once painted a picture during a
group performance in 1961. Jean
Tiguely had built a mechanical stripper for this happening, a machine
that jumped about on stage discard-
ing metal parts, Jasper Johns contributed a target made of flowers, and
Niki de Saint-Phalle had a marksman
shoot at one of her works. Rauschenberg's two-part work *Stripper* is pos-
sibly a pictorial response to the happenings of his colleagues. The black
arrow in the right picture points to a

cross made of wire that is suspended
in front of the canvas. With the bent
square applied to the square format
of the right panel, Rauschenberg was
alluding ironically to Albers' series
"Homage to the Square." The canvas-
es for *Stripper* were taken from two
of the pictures from the "White Paintings" series of 1951.

In 1962 Rauschenberg started to
take an interest in lithography. His in-
terests soon extended to include silk-
screen printing, as also used by Andy
Warhol, which permitted the enlarg-
ing of motifs to any size required.
With silk-screen printing, Rauschenberg discovered a medium which
continually allowed for new combinations and effects created by over-
lapping images and also made it possible for him to widely circulate his
artistic ideas. This may be seen in the
combined use of silk-screen printing
and everyday objects in *The Frightened Gods of Fortune.* Three picture

Robert Rauschenberg

born 1925
lives in Captiva, Florida

The Frightened Gods of
Fortune   1981
Wood, iron, collage
13 ft. x 16 1/4 in. x 6 ft.
The Marx Collection, owned by the
state of Berlin

planes are placed be-
tween the rungs of a lad-
der. The first American
president, George
Washington, looks gravely
out onto the world. It is
possible that the lurking
poisonous snake could be
caught with the lasso, but
finally, death seems un-
avoidable. The hands of
clocks are ticking; magni-
fied insects hint at the possible mutations caused by
an atomic war.

During the 1970s and
1980s, when the fear of
atomic war was at its
greatest, Rauschenberg
tried to confront these
anxieties with confidence-building
measures. In 1984, the ROCI (Rauschenberg Overseas Culture Inter-
change) was founded, an organiza-
tion aimed at improving relations
between peoples from different

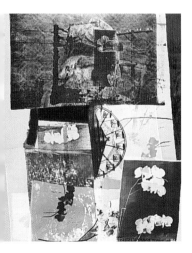

countries through cultural exchange.
Red China Green House is a collection of photographs from a trip
Rauschenberg took to China which
sowed in him the seeds of the idea to
found ROCI. This work belongs to
the "Salvage" series. "Salvage"
means to collect, to make use of, to
fully exploit, but also has the meaning of rescuing, recovering; this
generic term sums up the spirit of
Rauschenberg's concept of work and
the world. Rauschenberg is carrying
out a gigantic picture-recycling operation and, beyond this, is becoming
the "salvator mundi," the savior of
the world.   *D.S.*

Robert Rauschenberg   born 1925
lives in Captiva, Florida

Red China Green House   1984
Acrylic, collage on canvas
64 x 51 1/4 in.
The Marx Collection

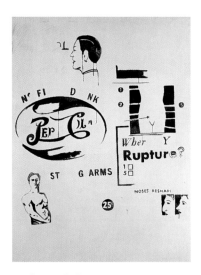

Andy Warhol   1928–87

Advertisement   1960

Acrylic, wax crayon on canvas
72 x 54 in.

The Marx Collection

From 1945 to 1949, Andy Warhol studied at the Carnegie Institute of Technology in Pittsburgh. In 1952 he moved to New York and worked there as a commercial artist and illustrator. The first independent art works date from 1960. These are based on banal motifs taken from comic strips or on mass-produced, and through advertising most widely circulated, images ranging from cans of soup to portraits of stars and press photographs of spectacular accidents. In the first years, Warhol still painted his preferred motifs by hand although he tried to avoid anything approaching an individual style. *Advertisement* of 1960 is one of the earliest examples, which Warhol continued to use in shop window displays. In accordance with Pop Art ideology, he challenged traditional concepts of art and originality. By using silkscreen printing techniques, which Warhol also employed in his can as pictures, he achieved an appearance of something mass-produced.

Warhol consciously concealed any signs of individuality and individual artistic ability. One of Warhol's early pictures in The Marx Collection, *Do it yourself (Seascape)*

Andy Warhol   1928–87

Do It Yourself (Seascape)   1962

Acrylic, pencil, transfer numbers on canvas   54 ¹/₂ x 72 in.

The Marx Collection

Andy Warhol   1928–87

Ambulance Disaster   1963

Silk screen, acrylic on canvas
10 1/4 x 6 1/2 ft.

The Marx Collection

from 1962, deals with the task of reproducing a picture by machine-like
repetition according to instructions.
The method of painting, a brainless
copying of a trivial motif, not only al-
ludes ironically to the supposed aura
of the original painting, but also ele-
vates the original, seemingly devoid
of any subjectivity, to the level of
uniqueness. In other examples from
this series of four pictures, the painted areas have numbers whereas the
blank areas have none — an absurd
reversal of the idea of painting a
copy according to instructions.

After the enlarged paint-by-num-
bers pictures from an amateur's
paint-box, the series of the Campbell's soup can, the one-dollar bills,
and the stickers for transporters
("Handle with care — Glass —
Thank you," 1962), the leap to the
"Disaster" pictures is shocking. *Ambulance Disaster* from 1963 shows,
for example, the terrifying absurdity

of violence as a part of everyday life.
It is violence that within seconds is
capable of completely reversing established roles. Warhol said of his
motives behind creating pictures of
death: "I believe it was the picture of
the airplane crash [and its headline]
on the cover of the magazine: '129
Die.' I was painting the Marilyns at
the same time. I realized that everything I do is connected to death….
But if you keep on seeing a horrific
image, it will eventually lose its terror." Through the reproduction of
terrifying images in the mass media,
the public eventually becomes de-
sensitized to images of violence and
consequently to the suffering of others. By doubling the picture, Warhol
suggested the use of this sort of photography for spectacular effect. The
image receives a new designation
through this artistic transformation as
well as through its new, public setting. The realistic context of the inci-

Andy Warhol   1928–87

Campbell's Soup Can   1965

Silk screen, acrylic, aluminum paint on
canvas   36 x 24 1/4 in.

The Marx Collection

Andy Warhol   1928–87

Twenty Jackies 1964

Silk screen, acrylic on
canvas   6 3/4 x 6 3/4 ft.

The Marx Collection

gous to the production of merchandise — to prevent sensitivity to the mass product, he still succeeds in retaining the drama of this unique situation and above all in not degrading Jackie Kennedy. Just as in his famous Monroe series, the emphasis is not on anonymity and the subject's mask-like quality, as is so often maintained, but rather on the inherent monumentality of an icon propagated by the media. Warhol tried in his portraits to tap into the source of power possessed by these designs.

dent is redefined in the museum; the sensational press photograph is reinstated as a work of art.

The series *Twenty Jackies* of 1964 also deals with the theme of death. Warhol, like millions of other Americans, was deeply affected by the murder of John F. Kennedy. He elevated the grieving Jackie Kennedy as the superstar of a drama which, like all other products of our society, had been mercilessly marketed. Despite the inherent idea behind this series, which is — by using repetition analo-

The enormous portrait entitled *Mao* is based on the photograph that was used as a frontispiece in Mao Tse-Tung's writings. Warhol respected, as it were, the idealized image of the communist leader — an image belonging to a particular ideological context — and placed it in the western context of the superstar, from Marilyn Monroe and Elvis Presley to Mick Jagger. Just as the enormous visual popularity of the Cuban revolutionary, Che Guevara, was founded upon the wide circulation of one photograph, so, in his "Mao" series,

Andy Warhol   1928–87

Shadow Painting 1978

Silk screen, acrylic on canvas
6 1/2 x 13 1/2 ft.

The Marx Collection

Andy Warhol   1928–87

Mao   1973
Silk screen, acrylic on canvas
14 $^3/_4$ x 11 $^1/_4$ ft.
The Marx Collection

Warhol achieves the enthronement of Mao as a pop idol by artistically assimilating the powers inherent in this cliché. In his Mao pictures, Warhol once again used painterly elements that transgress areas which had remained monochrome in the backgrounds of earlier portraits. A series of paintings executed in 1978 diverged completely from Warhol's previous work. They totally break away from representational and photographic elements, and possess an abstract character untypical of Warhol. Among the first series are the so-called "Oxidation Paintings," which the artist created by urinating on a mixture of metal and pigment

Andy Warhol   1928–87

Untitled   1956

Ballpoint pen on chamois-colored
drawing paper   16 3/4 x 14 in.

The Marx Collection

other representational groups of
work based on photographic details.
They are most closely related to an
untitled series from 1984 known as
the "Rorschach series," so called because they were made with the blot-
ting transfer method developed by
the psychiatrist Rorschach, which
often produces random, butterfly-
like shapes. The "Shadow Paintings"
are different in their visual character.
One series, dating from 1978, shows
an angular shadow form in different
color combinations. In 1979, Warhol
exhibited these pictures strung together rather like a ribbon which
opened up the space in a strange
way. The picture from The Marx Collection communicates rather a painterly impression reminiscent of a mis-
ty landscape bathed in diffused light.

powder placed on a canvas. Warhol
used other unusual media in his
paintings such as melted chocolate
and strawberry jam. In some ways,
the "Oxidation Paintings" are less
representational than the "Shadow
Paintings" whose very title suggests
the depiction of particular things. The
"Shadow Paintings" evolved as individual images or a series of images
until 1988, and were in no way expressions of an abstract phase in
Warhol's work. They stand alongside

The Marx Collection contains a
significant group of drawings from
the 1950s. Warhol had early on developed a sort of monotype by trac-
ing pencil drawings onto tissue paper
in ink and subsequently making a
print on watercolor paper. This process, also used in a similar way by
Paul Klee, enabled Warhol to re-fit
parts of his drawings into different
contexts. This simple form of transfer
printing already contained the key
elements that Warhol later employed
in his series of images using silk-
screen printing. He succeeded for
the first time in blurring the distinction between original and reproduction. The themes of these early draw-

Andy Warhol   1928–87

Golden Portrait   1957

Gold leaf, watercolor on white card
(transfer print)
22 3/4 x 15 3/4 in.

The Marx Collection

ings also already anticipate the later works' motifs taken from everyday life.

Although Warhol was a highly talented draftsman, as can be seen in his early drawings, later in his career he almost exclusively worked with reproductions, in particular photographs taken from newspapers and his own Polaroid shots.

In 1963, Warhol bought a 16 mm camera and shot his first film *Sleep*. In the same year, he moved into his new studio at 231 East 47th Street in New York which would become known as "the Factory." In 1965, just as he was being hailed as the most influential Pop artist, Warhol announced the end of his painting career. Fascinated by the electronic reproduction of film images, which intrude daily into the private lives of millions of people, Warhol wanted to dedicate himself completely to the medium of film. In association with film maker Paul Morrissey, whom he met in 1965, Warhol made many joint films during the following period starring friends and acquaintances from the Factory circle (e.g. *My Hustler*). In 1964, Warhol had already filmed the Empire State Building over a 24-hour period, making visible only the relentless passage of time. The work on the film *Flesh* began in July 1968, and in 1969 Warhol and Morrissey filmed *Trash* with Joe Dallesandro in the main role.

Andy Warhol 1928–87

Interview

Magazine year 1, no. 11, July 1970
11 3/4 x 8 1/2 in.

Kunstbibliothek, acquired 1992

The first copy of *Interview* appeared in the same year, published by Gerald Malanga, Morrissey, Warhol, and John Wilcock. One of the covers of this magazine shows Warhol in his typical pose as a photographer. The camera was his constant companion, an instrument which he used to create distance between himself and his environment. Yet it enabled him to record and closely observe these surroundings before further exploiting them in his pictures. *E.B.*

Andy Warhol 1928–87

Interview

Magazine year 3, no. 28,
December 1972
11 3/4 x 17 in.

Kunstbibliothek, acquired 1992

Roy Lichtenstein   born 1923
lives in Southampton, New York

The Melody Haunts My Reverie
1965

Color silk screen   27 x 23 in.

Kupferstichkabinett, acquired 1971

Even the most widely diverging attitudes within the Pop Art world were reunited in their desire to assimilate the aesthetic appeal of the industrial and consumer society along with its accompanying mass culture. The Pop artists picked up on realistic and surrealistic traditions as well as on the inventions of the Neo-Dadas. Although strongly influenced by these ideas, Roy Lichtenstein stayed within the boundaries of traditional painting and sculpture while shattering their conventions with his unusual subject matter. By the end of the 1950s his paintings, which then owed a lot to Abstract Expressionism, included comic strip figures as an ironical comment on that style of painting. By elevating comic strips to an art form, Lichtenstein returned to figurative painting in a highly unusual way. He used the impersonal, stereotyped lines that define figures and separat-

ed areas of color from areas of halftone dots to develop a mechanical style of painting divorced from an emotional approach to color.

In Lichtenstein's work, the clearly contoured representation and its banal narrative subject matter, as well as the composition, built on an abstract concept of form in which every line and area are calculated exactly, are the elements of a paradoxical relationship. It is this same ambiguity which has enabled him since about 1963 to transfer his comic style onto classic works of modern art, such as those by Picasso, among others.

In *Femme dans un fauteuil*, Lichtenstein has reworked the linear basic structure of the figure from Picasso's 1943 *Femme assise dans un fauteuil* as if it were a drawing from a comic strip. The lines, and the areas of color they so sharply define, do not betray an individual artist's handwriting. Lichtenstein purposely worked with Magna paints which can be completely removed with turpentine so as to destroy all traces of alterations or pentimenti.

Within Lichtenstein's oeuvre, *Coastal Village* belongs to a series of landscape pictures which are more concerned with an analysis of the brushstroke than with depicting landscape. The coastal scene with house, beach, boats, trees, and clouds disappears behind a typology of brushstrokes. Every one of these great sweeps of the paintbrush was sketched beforehand, its course plotted exactly. The styles range from comic-like brushstrokes, clear contours filled in with color to strokes which seem spontaneously applied, making an expressive impression.

The parallel diagonal lines depicting the sky between layers of cloud

Roy Lichtenstein

born 1923
lives in Southampton,
New York

Femme dans un fauteuil
1963

Oil, magna on canvas
5 $^3/_4$ x 4 ft.

The Marx Collection

are reminiscent of forms used by
Lichtenstein in his mirror pictures to
suggest the reflection of light.

E.B.

Roy Lichtenstein   born 1923
lives in Southampton, New York

Coastal Village   1987

Oil, magna on canvas
7 x 10 ft.

The Marx Collection

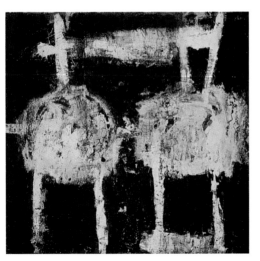

Cy Twombly   born 1928
lives in Lexington, Gaeta, and Rome

Untitled   1951
Bitumen, emulsion paint on canvas
4 x 4 ¹/₂ ft.
The Marx Collection

Cy Twombly, who has lived mainly in
Rome since 1957, certainly occupies
an exceptional position among the
great American artists of today.
Under the influence of the New
York school, and having critically
explored the art of Jackson Pollock
and Robert Rauschenberg, Twombly
developed a language of painting
which contains the double-edged
symbolism of both description and eradication, reve-
lation and concealment.
The earliest picture in the
Marx Collection, *Untitled*,
dates from 1951, from his
student days at Black

Mountain College. The
picture is painted over
a work by Robert Raus-
chenberg and shows
two similar, light forms
against a dark back-
ground, joined together
by an elongated hori-
zontal form of the same
chromatic tone. These
almost circular shapes
are reminiscent of the
works of Twombly's
contemporaries Robert
Motherwell and Franz
Kline, and also of fig-
ures produced long be-
fore these by primitive
cultures whose simplic-
ity and symbolism were significant
not only for Twombly. As he put it,
his art developed out of an "interest
in abstraction as well as humanist
symbols."

These originally rigid symbols become visibly more mobile and transform themselves, as we can observe
in *Free Wheeler*. This work was
painted in the summer of 1955 in
New York. Pencil and crayon lines
run across the light background
almost as if they are being gently
drawn to the top right corner, a pecu-
liarity of the force of direction in
Twombly's paintings to the present
day. These lines, occasionally stabi-
lized and held in place by areas of

Cy Twombly   born 1928
lives in Lexington, Gaeta, and
Rome

Free Wheeler   1955
Emulsion paint, wax crayon,
colored crayon, pencil, pastel
on canvas   5 ³/₄ x 6 ¹/₄ ft.
The Marx Collection

Cy Twombly born 1928
lives in Lexington, Gaeta, and
Rome
Untitled 1986
Part I: Wax crayons on canvas
4 x 3 ¹/₄ ft.
Part II: Oil on canvas
15 ³/₄ x 19 ³/₄ in.
The Marx Collection

over-painting, advance
across the surface like a
moving and multi-layered
net. From time to time they
take on the appearance of
writing exercises, although
they remain illegible. We
are not yet sure if writing is
suitable as an instrument of
communication or if the
world could also be ade-
quately described by the
flow of lines.

In *Empire of Flora*, painted in Rome in 1961, a
flesh-like quality predomi-
nates. The artist sometimes
used his fingers to create
this picture which shows
warm flesh tones and red,
pink, yellow, and brown patches. It
reflects the experiences of the American in Rome — in a new environment in which graffiti exist alongside
Baroque ceiling frescoes. Referring
to a passage from Ovid's *Metamor-
phoses*, Heiner Bastian recalls the
moment of man's transformation into
flowers which is represented in *Empire of Flora*. With this allusion in
mind, it is possible for the viewer to
recognize analogies of a breast and a
rose in the picture. Death, or more
precisely, the dismembering of the
body, is the temporary state revealed
to us in this image. The cheerful
mood it nevertheless exudes is also
due to its rosy tonality, which does
not reappear in Twombly's work until
the 1980s; now, however, it appears
in a more fluid and coherent form
than in *Untitled* from 1986, in which

the glowing red veils seem to pay
homage to a sumptuous view of
nature along the lines of William
Turner or Claude Monet. But behind
the beauty manifested here in a
seductive haze of color hides a potential catastrophe. The veils can
imperceptibly transmute from the
warmth of the sun and showers of
flowers into the heat of fire and
bloodlust. There is no evidence that
Twombly has more trust in nature
than he has in the body.   *A.S.*

Cy Twombly   born 1928
lives in Lexington, Gaeta, and Rome

Empire of Flora   1961

Oil, wax crayon, color crayon, pencil on
canvas   6 $^1/_2$ x 8 ft.

The Marx Collection

View of the East Gallery

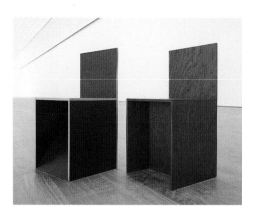

Donald Judd   1928–94

Two Chairs   1991–92

Mahogany plywood/plywood painted
green   30 x 15 x 15 in.

Kunstgewerbemuseum, acquired 1995

The painter, sculptor, architect, and
furniture-designer Donald Judd, born
in Excelsior Springs, Missouri, was
one of the major and, at the same
time, most controversial advocates of
a new art which disassociated itself
from the philosophies and visual traditions of Europe. Together with Jack-

Donald Judd   1928–94

Untitled   1966–77

Galvanized iron, aluminum
3 $^1/_4$ x 15 $^3/_4$ x 3 $^1/_4$ ft.

The Marx Collection

son Pollock, Barnett New-
man, Frank Stella, Ken-
neth Noland, and Richard
Serra, he shared a view of
art as something funda-
mental and relevant to the
times and to the experi-
ence of living. Donald
Judd, although continually
associated with Minimal
Art, rejected this term, as
he did all stylistic clichés.
His vision was more de-
manding and at the same
time more modest. He
wanted to create simple and clear
things that demand analysis. He
envisaged a unity of art, life, and
nature, which he was also later able
to put into practice in Marfa, Texas.

He first began as a painter in
1960–61, turning to the creation of
objects in 1962. Along with Dan
Flavin, who shared many of his opin-
ions, he avoided the word "sculpture," since he was "only interested
in those things that define space."
His objects are either attached to the
wall or stand or lie on the floor. For
the most part they consist of identical
elements arranged above or next to
each other, which he did not con-
ceive of as a structure or parts merely
lined up in a row, but as a unity, as a
whole. Symmetry was not an important factor for him but rather, as he

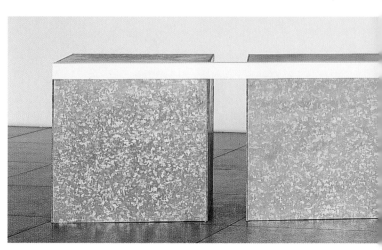

Donald Judd   1928–94

Untitled   1985

Aluminum, plexiglass
10 parts: each 6 x 27 x 24 in.

The Marx Collection

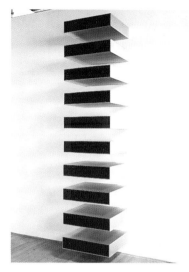

explained in a lecture at Yale University in 1989, proportion. His instructions for exhibitions are very precise. In works composed of individual small elements attached to the wall or frame-like structures standing on the floor, the intervals between objects correspond to the size of the objects. In the rows of cubes, the distance between the cubes constitutes a quarter of the length of one of their edges, and for pieces attached horizontally to the wall, the height of the upper edge must be five feet, just below eye-level. For both the wall pieces and the floor objects, the view into or onto the works was crucial for Judd since a particular perspective not only takes in the whole visually, but also points to distinctions between interior and exterior. In late works especially, the interior spaces are often colored, giving the impression that the inner volume is larger or at least different from that suggested by the outside shape.

Judd began to design furniture, too. In this, he was aided not only by the distinction he made between the non-functional nature of his art and the functionality of architecture and of furniture created for use, but also by his conviction, already expressed in *Arts Magazine* of 1964, "that forms of art and of non-art have always had a relationship with one another." Only when there is this harmony between all things has one world come into being.   *D.H.*

Dan Flavin   1933–96

Untitled   1996
Blue and green fluorescent neon tubes
Nationalgalerie, acquired 1996

The public's fascination in the way Flavin´s installation has radically altered the appearance of the Hamburger Bahnhof lies in the simplicity of the work. Blue neon tubes mounted on the building's façade and the historical building linking the Ehrenhof wing are set off against internal green neon lighting. Standard off-the-shelf tubes installed opposite each other, one color on the inside, another on the outside. What "you see [is] what you get" is Flavin's ironic and disillusionary comment on his own art. The effect, however, is startling. The aloofness of Prussian architecture of the late neo-classical revival period is transformed into a

three-dimensional picture of light in which the regal quality of blue encompasses the intimacy of green in its secret aura. By moving closer to the installation the viewer is bathed in the colored light and, as such, becomes part of the work of art. The play of light on the building's architecture continuously creates new areas of color through which the visitor passes. Beginning with Caspar David Friedrich's *Monk by* *the Sea* and moving past the captivating colors of Barnett Newman's work, the visitor reaches the flood of color in Flavin's contemporary light installation.   *P.K.S.*

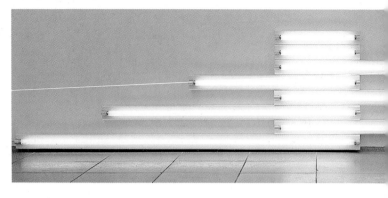

Dan Flavin 1933–96

Untitled (Monument to V. Tatlin)
1968

8 white fluorescent neon tubes
32 in. x 14 ft. x 4 ¹/₂ in.
Nationalgalerie, acquired 1995

As early as 1963, Dan Flavin created an installation of diagonally arranged fluorescent light tubes on the wall of his New York atelier, aiming "to produce a cheerful and restless neon picture that, by irradiating its physical presence, almost dissolves into invisibility." He dedicated it to Brancusi. He was not interested in the production of a body or a surface, but in an immaterial, and yet visually perceptible spatial manifestation advancing to the outer reaches of visibility. In this, Flavin did not want to create "icons," as he termed them, which meant anthing or referred to anything beyond themselves. Instead he invented images of space that would be self-contained and freed from any materiality — images which would disassociate themselves completely from the triviality of the mass-produced objects which the artist had used to create them. In order to do this, he does not use individual and isolated light-objects but continually seeks already existing spaces and those which — like his materials — were made for totally different purposes. It is especially in these spaces with previous associa-

tions that the transforming power of his manipulations is made clear.

Flavin creates works that have to be observed. And it is exactly in this process of recognition, when the viewer becomes weary of the significance of the representation or contents, that images are created which have no explanation and no dependence on anything else, and consist only of themselves. This vision of pure vividness thrown back upon itself has produced new conditions for observation, as well as for the object itself. The Marx Collection contains some of Flavin's important works such as *Two Primary Series and One Secondary* (1968) and *Untitled* (1978), which can now be shown together with *Untitled* (1968) from the Nationalgalerie.

Dan Flavin created expressly for the Hamburger Bahnhof a work which completely responds to the architectural setting it was made for; it binds together the exterior and interior of the building as well as its connecting passages. In addition to linking objects in the collection, the artist gives the inside and the outside of the building a look relevant to his ideas.

Even if we had to reach an agreement about what it is that Dan Flavin really creates, we see that it is not least by his working with the architecture of the Hamburger Bahnhof that we comprehend a visual quality freed from the architectural parameters set by the new function of this

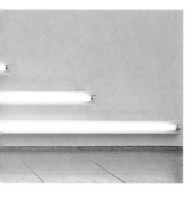

Dan Flavin 1933–96

Untitled 1968–69

Red, yellow, and green fluorescent neon
tubes 48 x 4 ¹/₄ x 3 ¹/₂ in.

The Marx Collection

Dan Flavin 1933–96

Untitled 3 1978

Pink, green, yellow, and blue fluorescent
neon tubes 48 x 48 x 8 in.

The Marx Collection

structure. The whole building opens
itself to this new philosophy; it represents a historical condition, but at
the same time also its present state
which, although so unusual, appeals
to the viewer. Flavin does not define
space, but rather the openness produced during observation, the cross-
ing of borders of the idea conceived
in the visual perception. Since visual
perception does not require a physical object nor contents communicated by objects, Flavin's art is freed
from the search for unrelated inter-
pretations. The content and the object of Flavin's art is visual perception
itself, and no more than what it is
able to bring forth. This absolute
liberation of art from all limitations
and definitions, including material
circumstances, gives Flavin his
special standing. His work consists
of nothing more than the art of producing meaning from meaningless
materials.   *D.H.*

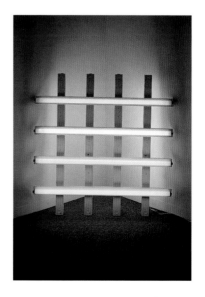

Mario Merz born 1925
lives in Turin

La Goccia D'Aqua (The Drop of
Water) 1987
Metal tubes, glass, neon numbers
2 $^1/_2$ x 86 $^3/_4$ x 14 $^1/_2$ ft.
Nationalgalerie, acquired 1994

Since the late 1960s igloos, tables,
and Fibonacci numbers (an infinite
numerical sequence in which each
number represents the sum of the
two numbers preceding it, as in
1,1,2,3,5,8,13 etc.) have been essential elements of Mario Merz's work.
In continually new forms and combinations with, on the one hand, the
written word and, on the other hand,
real objects, he uses basic and raw
materials such as earth, glass, metal,
and neon to create precisely outlined
and transparent spaces which con-
dense poetic and philosophical
thoughts on life — in this scientific

and technological age which knows no boundaries.

In comparison to the early igloos, *La Goccia D'Aqua* seems cool and hermetic, an impression heightened by the presence of thin neon numbers. Combined with the cap-like glass form, they refer to arithmetical systems, series of numbers, and the progression of time. The transparent and fragile dome can also be interpreted as a metaphor for the human brain and its ability to think. The igloo is pierced by an eighty-two-foot-long metal table shaped like an arrow-head with a water tap attached to its tip. The sounds of gurgling and dripping water bring movement to the frozen and rigid objects, promising new life.   *A.S.*

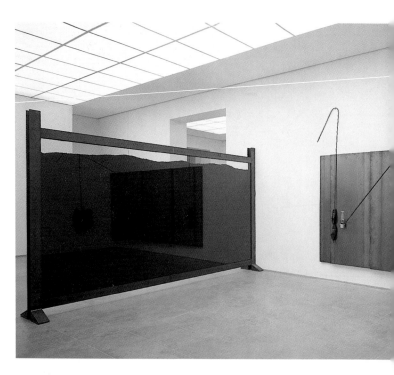

Jannis Kounellis   born 1936
lives in Rome
Senza titolo (Untitled)   1989
Wall of coffee beans, steel wall, oil
lamp, sack of coal, metal plates, shoes
8 ³/₄ x 14 ft., 7 ³/₄ x 14 ¹/₄ ft.
Nationalgalerie, acquired 1990 by the Preussischer
Kulturbesitz and the state of Berlin with proceeds
from the German Lottery, Berlin.

This work, which like so many others has no name, shows an assemblage of a glass wall filled with coffee beans, four steel sheets, a sack
of coal, an oil lamp, and the worn
shoes of the artist. Both formally
and in regard to its content, it recalls the works Kounellis developed during the late 1960s in
the context of Arte Povera. The
aromatic wall of coffee beans,
evoking vital energy while at the
same time suggesting a barren
landscape, forms the entrance to
this room. Opposite it hangs a sack
of coal containing, in contrast with
the small, smooth coffee beans,
larger, and rougher, lumps of coal.
The sack takes on the form of a tor-

so. The six-foot-high and two-foot-
wide sheets of steel overlap one
another and are screwed in place
at right angles to the coffee wall.
They correspond to measurements
that Kounellis frequently used in
his works with bedsteads in 1969.
As the place of birth, procreation,
death, and suffering, they refer to
life's various stations and limited
duration. The division of the steel
wall into four parts represents the
four stages of life, a symbolism that
is emphasized by the artist's worn-
out shoes. The left shoe is placed in
front of the right, corresponding to
the traditional stance of a Greek
kouros. The significant absence of
a person here reflects the absence
of the artist as well as that of Apol-
lo, the god of light and the arts,
who takes on many forms in Kounellis' work.
   Just as the lamp held by the female figure throws light on the full
horror of the event in Picasso's
Guernica, the peaceful flame of
domesticated fire here refers to the

Robert Morris   born 1931
lives in New York

Felt-Piece   1970

Felt   9 $^1/_4$ x 13 ft.

Nationalgalerie, acquired 1982 by the Preussischer Kulturbesitz and the state of Berlin with proceeds from the German Lottery, Berlin.

Robert Morris is considered to be one of the most important theoreticians of Minimal Art although he cannot be described as a purely minimalist artist. His artistic development led from happenings and Pop Art in the early 1960s to experimentation with different materials. Through his objects, the observer is confronted with phenomena that are aesthetic to his perception. The *Felt-Piece* belongs to a series of works executed in felt, in which Morris experimented with the soft material. He was interested in the material's simple structure and how it behaved under different conditions. Taking the strongly expressive qualities of the felt as a starting point, he achieved a variety of visual forms and integrated a concept of the viewer's perceptive possibilities into his work.   *B.S.*

absence and dismemberment of man, and once more throws doubt on the civilizing achievements of our society.   *A.S.*

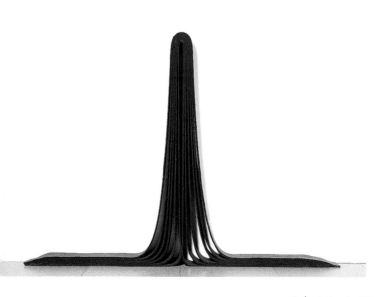

Richard Long born 1945
lives in Bristol

Berlin Circle 1996
Slate Diameter 40 ³/₄ ft.
The Marx Collection

Although having little interest in the art business, Richard Long, to this day an individualist in the truest sense of the word, made a breakthrough within a very few years. He cannot be classified as belonging to any one of the movements that developed in the late 1960s and 1970s. At the same time, however, his art absorbed something from the trends of those years: the "poor" and natural materials from Arte Povera, the way

of working directly in nature from Land Art, the reduced form from Minimal Art — and his wanderings in search of a concept of form have the character of a performance.

Richard Long is a globetrotter, who travels the world not to visit historical sites, but to wander through uninhabited and remote regions. And if these wanderings are not themselves already works of art, they inspire Long to create it: trodden lines, stone formations, spilled water. They are works that are taken from nature and return to nature, works that are owned by no one and that cannot be possessed, not even by the artist who documents them in photographic form: one work, one creator who is at the same time the only viewer, and one photographic document which makes it accessible to us all.

The unconditional character of the form and the modest requirements of its realization have a somewhat Franciscan and, at the same time, democratic feeling about them. Richard Long's work contains no hierarchies; each branch, each stone, every piece of turf remains as it is and, despite this, serves the needs of the whole. The pieces are not sculptures in the common meaning of the word as they form homogenous lines, paths, or discs. "My outdoor sculptures are places," says Long — places to spend time in and where even he can rest during his wanderings.

We find in Richard Long not only an artist, but another philosophy, another form of experience and life.   *D.H.*

Richard Long   born 1945
lives in Bristol

Sandstone Circle   1977

Stones   Diameter 13 ft.

Nationalgalerie, acquired 1977

John Cage   1912–92

Not Wanting to Say Anything about
Marcel   1969

Plexigrams I–VIII
each with 8 sheets of silk-screened
plexiglass, base made of walnut
14 $^1/_2$ x 14 $^1/_2$ x 24 in.

Nationalgalerie, acquired 1993 and 1996 with aid
from the René Sintenis Foundation

and

Lithographies A and B
(from *Not Wanting to Say Anything
about Marcel*) 1969

Lithographies on black paper
each 27 $^1/_2$ x 39 $^1/_2$ in.

Kupferstichkabinett, acquired 1996

Above: detail
Below: complete view of the installation

John Cage founded an experimental,
extended definition of music which
enabled him to compose unusual
pieces such as, in 1938, his first composition for a "prepared" piano.
Cage worked with artists, dancers,
and musicians, and developed performances which crossed the boundaries between different art forms.
He was not only friends with Marcel
Duchamp up to his death, but also
adapted his "Ready-Made" principle
as his own. In 1941, László Moholy-
Nagy invited Cage to the Chicago
School of Design to teach a class in
experimental music. In the late
1940s, Cage turned to eastern philosophies under the influence of the
Zen-Buddhist teacher Suzuki and
made the Chinese book of changes,
I Ching, the basis for his decision
making. The seemingly coincidental
operations resulting from this also
became part of his composing technique.

The death of Duchamp in 1968
inspired Cage to produce his first
sculpture, *Not Wanting to Say Anything about Marcel*. Together with
the designer Calvin Sumsion, he
made a multiple consisting of eight

plexigrams, which hints subtly at Duchamp's way of thinking (printed glass, a box as a container, etc.). Through the random arrangement of the writing and fragmentary images, Cage attempted to escape from all the influences of a conscious aesthetic order and the questions of taste connected to it. This object "that was of no importance" (J. Cage, 1984) finds its home somewhere near the phonetic poems of the Dadaists, but also not far from the word games of the Fluxus artists.

In the book accompanying the work, Cage wrote: "If one has a few questions to ask and requires many answers, an efficient way of proceeding is by programing a modern computer. If, on the other hand, one has many questions and needs only a few answers (as in the production of a work of art), it is more efficient to program oneself. The most ancient way of permitting an individual to program is provided by the mechanism of the *I Ching*.... Consequently, I based a dictionary on the *I Ching*; I chose words, then letters out of those words, and finally their spatial order at random. I distributed these words on pieces of plexiglass, taking their typology — which is also based on chance — into consideration. I placed the eight plexiglass panes parallel to each other on a wooden pedestal. The result is that the letters show up in depth; when you look

at them, they overlap and are connected...."

Cage did not start to paint until 1988, apart from his early attempts in the late 1920s and 1930s. In 1983 he began to experiment with watercolors, but it was not until a workshop five years later that he thoroughly explored this medium. The watercolor *Untitled* belongs to a series that he painted at the Miles C. Horton, Sr. Research Center in Mountain Lake, Virginia in 1988. In it, Cage refers to the spiritual order of the famous stone-garden of the Ryoan-ji Monastery in Kyoto, which he had visited several times. Once again, with help from the *I Ching*, Cage positioned fifteen stones on paper and then outlined them with a watercolor brush. Using different techniques, the artist produced several series of works in this way in an attempt to transform the secrets of the garden and of the book of wisdom.   *E.B.*

John Cage   1912–92
Untitled   1988
Watercolor on paper   18 $^{1}/_{2}$ x 36 in.
Kupferstichkabinett, acquired 1991

Cage's work, a somewhat destructive energy *(Hommage à John Cage, One for Violin)*. Paik turned to electronic media images as early as 1963. Using his specially reconstructed televisions, he was one of the first artists to distance himself by the use of irony from this medium of the masses.

When the firm Sony produced the first portable video recorder in 1965, Paik used the images relayed by television as an inexhaustible reservoir for his picture montages and manipulations.

The Nationalgalerie owns two reconstructed objects by Paik that were shown in his Wuppertal exhibition of 1963 entitled "Exposition of Music-Electronic Television": *Point of Light* and *Zen for TV*. With both video sculptures, which extinguish the electronically transmitted image and reduce it to a point or a line, Paik

Nam June Paik   born 1932
lives in New York

Zen for TV   1963 (1990)

Monitor   26 $^1/_2$ x 18 $^3/_4$ x 15 in.

Nationalgalerie, gift of the artist 1993

Nam June Paik, who studied music in Japan and Germany, moved to Europe in 1956 and to the USA in 1964. His art was influenced by John Cage's extended definition of music. Paik met Cage in Darmstadt in 1958. His first performances, created in the spirit of Fluxus art had, in contrast to

Nam June Paik   born 1932
lives in New York

Triangle: Video-Buddha und Video-Denker
(… and Video Thinker)   1976 (1991)

Closed circuit installation, 4 monitors, 2 video cameras, 2 sculptures, 2 tripods

Nationalgalerie, acquired 1993 by the Verein der Freunde der Nationalgalerie

Nam June Paik born 1932
lives in New York

Monument 1986
21 monitors, 2 video recorders, 2 video
tapes 12 x 14 1/4 x 1 3/4 ft.
Nationalgalerie, acquired 1988

registered early doubts about the supposedly progressive "information society." Paik made a comparison between the rationally incomprehensible quantities of information leading to spiritual limbo and the "emptiness" of meditation.

The idea of transforming the electronic medium creatively was continued in the work *Magnet TV* of 1965–91, in which the visitor is invited to create his own images with the aid of a magnet which interferes with the lines on the screen. The video sculpture *Monument*, which belongs to the "Family of Robots" series, transforms recorded fragments of images into rotating ornaments of color. They can be seen simultaneously on twenty-one screens that Paik installed in fifty-year-old television sets and then stacked up. The large-scale video sculpture *Triangle:*

Video-Buddha und Video-Denker brings together, in the sense of Eurasian thinking — which influenced Paik's friend Joseph Beuys — eastern and western culture in one medium. It demands not only a return to a meditative attitude, as did Paik's early works, but sees positive possibilities in the transforming quality of electronic image transmission. In several satellite transmissions that Paik organized, he did not merely attempt to present differing artistic viewpoints simultaneously, but also tried to make their artistic messages accessible to as many people as possible over large distances. Rodin's *Thinker*, the embodiment of western philosophy, is just as much at the mercy of the electronic medium as Buddha, whose meditative self-absorption directly opposes the superficiality inherent in the medium of the masses.   *E.B.*

George Maciunas   1931–78

Fluxus-1   1964

Diverse Fluxus objects in envelopes with stuck-on leporellos and metal screw fittings in a wooden box
8 ³/₄ x 9 ¹/₂ x 2 in.

Kunstbibliothek, acquired 1990

Taking John Cage's ideas as a starting point, in 1961 the designer George Maciunas, who originated from Lithuania, developed a strategy for cultural revolution under the appealing slogan "Fluxus." As a US soldier stationed in Wiesbaden in 1962, Maciunas first organized concert-events in Europe and built up a sales agency for multiples. The mechanisms of the art market were to be undermined by small, usable, limited-edition objects, by collective presentation, and a self-organized sales agency. In line with this, *Fluxus-1* represents a lucky grab bag bursting with all sorts of surprises. The individual components, works by Joe Jones, Ay-O, Dick Higgins, George Brecht, and others, were varied as soon as one element became unavailable, and offered as a new edition. Maciunas soon perfected the outward appearance by — in reference to Marcel Duchamps' *boîte en valise* — circulating black briefcases as "Fluxkits."   *D.S.*

Wolf Vostell   born 1932
lives in Berlin

Elektronischer dé-coll/age Happening Raum (Electronic dé-coll/age Happening Room; detail)   1968–82

Glass, monitors, electronics, motors, mixed media

Nationalgalerie, acquired 1983 with proceeds from the German Lottery, Berlin

Wolf Vostell, one of the German Fluxus activists, came across the word "décollage" during a stay in Paris in 1954. It became the central theme for his artistic work. In Vostell's way of writing it, the sense of the word — division, separation — is also communicated visually. With "dé-coll/age," the artist defines his age as a torn one. Vostell's works and happenings are meant to mirror this meaning in their style and appearance.

Working consciously in the traditions of the Futurists and Dadaists in the 1950s, Vostell operated along parallel lines to Raymond Hains and Jacques de la Villeglé, who ripped down posters from billboards.

Public advertising space was discovered — before Nouveau Réalisme — as a place for art. Posters that had been stuck on top of one another were stripped away and displayed anew as multi-layered images. The subversive character of this sort of happening was emphasized by Vostell in 1959 when he stuck a National Socialist proclamation in his sketch book — a proclamation warning that acts of sabotage through the tearing down of posters would be punished by death. By the end of the 1950s Vostell began designing concepts for happenings and illustrating them in collaged scores. In the beginning, he gave stage directions (e.g. "Shout 'Wirtschaftswunder,' loud"), later he transported his audience in busses to different locations and exposed them to disturbing impressions (e.g. the squashing of a Mercedes between two locomotives in Wuppertal in 1963, or the screaming of jet engines at the military airport in Ulm in 1964).

The *Elektronischer dé-coll/age Happening Raum*, shown at the 1968 Venice Biennale, was also designed to provoke. Standing on a floor covered with pieces of broken glass, the viewers form part of the work with their movements as they activate the objects by triggering the photoelectric cells. Distorted — décollaged — television images, light and movement effects, the hissing of the televisions, rattling chains and shovels, a white cloth waving to and fro and, towering over everything, a bomb, are evidence of the political concern at the time of the Vietnam War.

The confrontation of our senses with the unavoidably complementary factors of war and the pressures of a consumer society are the main concerns of Vostell's oeuvre. Vostell sees his "artistic treatment of destruction as a permanent accusation." Here, the lightness and wit of the American Fluxus works have been replaced by a scenario of serious, teutonic agitation.   *D.S.*

Dieter Roth   born 1930
lives in Basel and Iceland

Buch für Kinder (Book for Children)
Reykjavík forlag ed.   1957
38 pages with spiral-binding
12 1/2 x 12 1/2 in.
Kunstbibliothek, acquired 1990

The artistic books by Dieter Roth,
which he himself calls "Buchver-
zweigungen" (book ramifications),
and which he considers to be his
main work, began in the 1950s with
Concrete Poetry. For the magazine

material, edited by Daniel Spoerri
and written on a typewriter, Roth
designed issue number 2 (1959). Its
square pages already indicate some
main features of his *Concrete Poetry*:
the page, black or white, is cut into
or has a piece missing, is perforated,
folded, divided up geometrically
with lines; it shows writing and written symbols in differing constellations, used sparingly or to cover
surfaces, forming graphic patterns
or remaining isolated. The programmatic poems with spellings especial-

Dieter Roth   born 1930
lives in Basel and Iceland

Poetrie

Hans Jörg Mayer Edition,
Stuttgart 1967
Book of plastic bags, printed
on both sides, plexiglass
book cover and screw-
binding   16 pages
Ex.1/7, luxury edition with
original clouding
11 x 5 1/2 in.
Kunstbibliothek, acquired 1990

ly invented by the artist are based on this procedure: "aine saite ler lasen/ si bekomt genvg bedoitvng fon andern saiten her vo etvas stet" (leave one page empty, it gets enough meaning from other pages where things are written).

Imaginative concepts for books followed in the 1960s, using collage materials as well as graphic elements.

Roth consciously allows time to play a role in his book objects. Organic substances such as foodstuffs, blood, mould, and glue — and the substances to which they are applied — eventually decompose, causing unpredictable changes. The "Literaturwürste" (literature-sausages) and the special edition of the magazine *poemetrie No. 4*, complete with minced mutton in a plastic bag, are examples of this. The special edition of *Poetri No. 1* (1967) made of the finest embossed and painted goat's leather, has been left to an uncertain fate through the effects of mould cultures.

In contrast to these are the technically perfect books produced by different printing processes which appeared first in "forlag ed." ("ed. publishing company") founded by himself, then later, and, above all, as Hansjörg Mayer editions. From the choice of the quality and color of the paper to the application of the medium, each one possesses its own individual character and uniqueness. Their common denominator is the defamiliarization caused by the reshaping and equalizing of all materials — whether it be on the level of the word, the picture, or the object. This is already expressed in the imaginative choice of materials for the covers of the special editions: corrugated paper with a squashed light bulb melted in plastic for the photo book "snow"; a brightly-colored silkscreen print with toy motifs for the comic and painting books *bok 3b* and *bok 3d*; oriental-like decorations on black faux leather for *bok 3a* with cuttings from Icelandic newspapers.

L.M.

Dieter Roth   born 1930
lives in Basel and Iceland

Collected Works
Vol. 7 *bok 3b, bok 3d,*
Vol. 12 *Copley Buch* (Copley Book)
Reconstruction, or rather extended version of the book published by the Copley Foundation 1961 and 1965
Hansjörg Mayer Edition, special edition, Stuttgart, London, Reykjavík   1974
9 x 6 3/4 in.

Kunstbibliothek, acquired 1990

Günter Brus   born 1938
lives on Gomera

Photograph from the 1st Happening
ANA   1964
11 1/2 x 15 1/2 in.
Nationalgalerie, acquired 1985

As a critical analysis of Art Informel, Günter Brus, Hermann Nitsch, and Otto Mühl developed an "Aktions-malerei" (performance painting) that was soon to go beyond the eruptive act of painting. One of the first happenings, in which a body fulfilled the role of the canvas, took place in Mühl's studio apartment in Oberen Augartenstraße in Vienna in 1964. In the opening sequence, Brus, who had painted all the walls and the ceiling white, rolled around the room, wrapped in cloth. He then painted his wife, Anni, and after that, the whole atelier.

In the following years, Brus became more radical in his use of the body as a material, and shocked the public with acts of self-mutilation. This provocative breaking of taboos by the Vienna happenings artists culminated in 1968 with the event "Kunst und Revo-

lution" (Art and Revolution) at the University of Vienna, where Brus maltreated his body with a razor, drank his own urine, and sang the Austrian national anthem while masturbating. In order to avoid a prison sentence, Brus fled to Berlin and, at Oswald Wiener's "Exil" restaurant, participated in the fictitious "Austrian Government in Exile" as "Emperor for Inner and Outer Affairs."   *D.S.*

Arnulf Rainer   born 1929
lives in Vienna

Darbringbietung (Performance-Offering)   1972–75
Dry point etching on zinc plate
20 3/4 x 27 1/2 in.
Kupferstichkabinett, acquired 1981

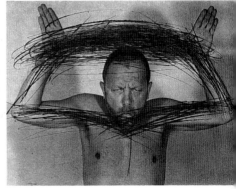

Arnulf Rainer   born 1929
lives in Vienna

Blaues Kreuz (Blue Cross)   1980–81
Etching   52 $^1/_2$ x 24 $^1/_2$ in.
Kupferstichkabinett, acquired 1982

Blaues Kreuz by Arnulf Rainer is the second image in a sequence of four etchings of crosses created between 1977 and 1986. Rainer continued the series in 1991 with a further two variations. The complete series can be found in this collection. It belongs to a series of works embarked on in 1953 in which overpainting and overdrawing later intensified into

"Zumalungen" (a complete covering of the background with paint). In a similar way, his early interest in his own physiognomy developed into his use of overdrawing in the *Darbringbietung*. In Rainer's own words, the aim of the "Zumalungen" is "laying-to-rest and mortification." In this process, the artistic act is "perhaps even more fundamental than the finished picture, for the participation in the step-by-step eclipsing or drowning of the image, its gradual sinking into the peace and invisibility (of the 'great ocean') may be compared with the attainment of contemplation in religious life," as referred to by the cross.

Each etching was printed in just one color since the "monochromatic use of color … is a royal path" to complete peace. With each phase, the darkened area of the cross grows and, in the last picture, the corner areas, which till now have been left uncovered, have been "laid to rest" by prints from four additional plates. In painting, the "mortification" of a single picture is often attained only through a process lasting many years. From a multitude of "movements and actions" has come "a single state of being; out of a plurality has come a single great emptiness." The medium of printing allows us to witness not only the last stages of the "laying-to-rest," but also the steps leading up to it, shedding light on the process itself and the temporary "plurality."   *A.D.*

Edward Kienholz 1927–94

Volksempfängers (People's Radios)
1975–77
Mixed media

Measurements vary according to construction
(Detail: Der Eisensockel; iron pedestal)

Nationalgalerie, acquired 1976 with aid from the state of Berlin

In September 1973, the American Edward Kienholz came to Berlin on a grant from the Deutscher Akademischer Austauschdienst (German Academic Exchange Service). Berlin became a second home to him, and he spent every winter here until his death. His artistic career began in the mid-1950s with painted wood reliefs. He combined assorted found objects and figures in ever-larger arrangements which he called "Tableaux." His first environment was *Roxy's*, a reconstruction of a bordello interior with two accessible rooms, which he completed in 1961. *Roxy's* — shown at the 1968 documenta in Kassel — made Kienholz famous in Europe. His first work in Berlin, with the ambiguous title "Still Life," also caused a stir: in a bourgeois home setting stood an armchair that the public could sit on. Aimed at it, however, was a device equipped with live cartridges and a random time switch. Reflections on everyday life and violence, the German state of mind and death are also important in the subsequent series, the "Volksempfängers."

The starting point for this was formed by two black radios from the 1930s which Kienholz had come across during his wanderings through the town and thought of as being typically German: "I really begin to understand any society by going through its junk stores and flea markets. It is a form of education and historical orientation for me. I can see the results of ideas in what is thrown away by a culture."

Kienholz was not so concerned with surrealistic effects but rather with a kind of "history from below" which he explored intuitively, not scientifically. This was the background to his creation, from January to June 1975, of the first eight (from a total of nineteen) assemblages of the "Volksempfängers." The presentation of these objects for use suggests human figures. This impression is strengthened by Kienholz's placement of the radios, with their connotations of maleness and associations with Hitlerian propaganda, alongside their female counterparts: washboards. The latter are decorated with "the German Mother's Cross of Honor" which Hitler awarded women for giving birth to four or more children of German blood.

The Nazis' ideological manipulation of everyday life included the use of music by Richard Wagner, which was often played during broadcasts for political occasions. Kienholz spontaneously associated his first "Volksempfängers" to Wagner's "The Valkyrie." He became more deeply involved in Wagner's music in February 1976, when he attended a performance of "The Rhinegold." The sculptures created after this refer to Wagner even in their titles *(The Norsemen, Notung, Brünhilde, The Rhine Maidens)*. Wagner's compositions can be turned on with a foot switch. The leitmotif of the giants from the second scene of "The Rhinegold" and "Sanft schloß Schlaf dein Aug'," for example, booms out of the "iron pedestal." By letting fragments from "The Ring of the Nibelung" sound out of the Volksempfängers, Kienholz brings together different levels of German history and mythology into one atmospherically dense complex.

A comment on the present is made in *Die Leiter* (The Ladder): a destroyed Volksempfänger is juxtaposed with the steering wheel of a Mercedes-Benz automobile, as a symbol of the affluence of post-war society. Torn between the failure of fascism and capitalism's potentially endless ladder of success, the German identity is symbolized by the loss of its center while still maintaining a connection through inner wires.

This sort of analysis can be explosive: in 1983 Edward and Nancy Kienholz won a competition organized by the Technische Universität, Berlin for the design of a fountain at Ernst-Reuter-Platz. The concept envisaged a Mercedes-Benz being slowly scrubbed away to scrap in a carwash. This view of things was not, however, politically acceptable.

D.S.

Gerhard Richter born 1932
lives in Cologne

Vorhang III (Hell) (Curtain III, light)
1965

Oil on canvas 6 1^{1}/$_{2}$ x 6 ^{1}/$_{2}$ ft.

Nationalgalerie, acquired 1975 with proceeds from
the German Lottery, Berlin

It had become impossible for many
artists in the period around and after
1960 to simply paint pictures. Abstract Expressionism had become a
rather stale convention and reality,
with happenings and Fluxus, was
forcing its way into art.

In 1962, Gerhard Richter turned
away from his previous painting style
and the abstract painting prevalent in
Europe. The concept of painting as
an idealistic, representational art
seemed to be dead, historically obso-
lete. Gerhard Richter, born in Dres-

den, originally painted stage sets in
Zittau before going to the Kunstakademie (Art Academy) in Dresden,
where he was trained as a "wall-
painter." In 1959, he visited the documenta 2 in Kassel, which made a
strong impression on him. Two
months before the Wall was built, he
emigrated from what was then East
Germany. He went to the Rhineland
area and matriculated at the
Düsseldorf Kunstakademie. Under
the tutelage of Karl Otto Goetz, himself an abstract painter, there was
plenty of freedom for the students to
develop, and it was here that Gerhard Richter and Sigmar Polke met.
This was the start of a stimulating and
productive friendship which inspired
both men to polemic attacks on the
conservative ideal of art, and which
led onwards to an extremely com-

plex development which revolution-ized art.

His first known paintings from 1962 were painted in a photo-realis-tic style. He borrowed his images from magazines, advertisements, books, private snapshots, and ama-teur photos. It was important to him that these images reflected everyday life, that he was working with ex-cerpts from reality "without style, without composition, and without previous judgement."

With the aid of an episcope pro-jector, he transferred the image onto the canvas, then applying the light and dark tones over it in thin glazes of oil paint. Because of the way the paintbrush glided over the surface of the paint, figures, objects, and spaces seem unfocused, veiled — similar to the images in a dream. Until 1965 Richter kept his photo-images exclu-sively in tones of gray. The choice of gray was a reaction against the strong colors used in Pop Art and New Real-ism then emerging in America. It was, at the same time, a logical choice: "Gray. It has absolutely no message, it gives off neither feelings nor associations, it is neither actually visible nor invisible. Its inconspicu-ousness makes it so suitable to medi-ate, to illustrate, in an illusionist way virtually the same as a photograph. And it is more suited than any other color to illustrate 'nothing'" (G. Richter, 1990).

As a model for his series of the gray "Vorhänge", he took the floor-

Gerhard Richter   born 1932

lives in Cologne

Seestück (Sea Piece)   1970

Oil on canvas   6 $\frac{1}{2}$ x 6 $\frac{1}{2}$ ft.

Nationalgalerie, acquired 1976 with proceeds from the German Lottery, Berlin

Gerhard Richter   born 1932
lives in Cologne

Atelier   1985
Oil on canvas
3 parts   each 8 ¹/₂ x 6 ¹/₂ ft.
Nationalgalerie, acquired 1985

length curtain in the still new, but influential gallery of Alfred Schmela in Düsseldorf. The theme underwent diverse variations. In the picture owned by the Nationalgalerie, the lower edge of the curtain is visible: this edge disappears in later versions which more strongly evoke the tube motif. The tube-like consistency of the folds takes on its own identity to such an extent that it begs comparison with corrugated iron rather than fabric. On closer observation, the illusion of an independent, relief-like skin of paint is achieved rather than an impression of photographic brilliance.

Since 1968 Richter has painted landscapes and sea and cloud studies. In the 1970 *Seestück*, the horizon divides the picture into two equal parts. There is no evidence of a hierarchy, and the use of gray tones throughout gives the picture an atmosphere of distancing indifference — indifference which mistrusts all things fixed, and which leaves space for hope that in its vagueness, the picture will open itself. Things we can see cause doubt. What is reality? But the images show only landscapes that afford just as little insight into reality as the curtain pictures. The subject matter is automatically examined for its message by the viewer. Purporting to be a documentation of reality, *Seestück* is immediately rejected by the viewer because it can only be read as a symbol, a painting which confuses our perception. This method of treating subjects in an unfamiliar way brings the photographed subject, often accepted as an understudy for reality, close to

abstract design. Richter entrusts the relationship between fiction and reality to perception.

The large picture *Atelier* from 1985 is one of the abstract "color explosions" which Richter has developed since 1983. While possessing freedom and spontaneity, the picture is still a "constructed" space with carefully composed forms and a structure based on more profound sources. Richter begins, as he himself noted, "quite harmlessly with any old structure and under no particular pretext; it is then painted over, painted out until something new and unknown is created." The clashing together of colors and forms bearing the title *Atelier*, the home of artistic activity, represents the existence of a painter completely floating on air. In its dizzying probing into what image is, what painting is, it intensifies almost into a painted drama. Layers of paint are revealed, applied over one another with a spatula, scraped away.

The impression of speed does not correspond to the act of painting, which is rather painstaking. Spaces and vistas have been created and the tube motif of the earlier curtain paintings has reappeared. Here, it does not divide, does not stabilize. It emerges in the middle of chaos and tectonics as if unable to bear the force released by the free areas of color. The painting is not an image of disintegration, but of the irregular dispersal of gestures and moods which have found visual expression. It offers an area of conflict for a reality which hides from us, evading definition. The dialogue between artist and viewer encourages critical and creative reflection on the supremacy of pictures.   *B.S.*

Sigmar Polke   born 1941

lives in Cologne

Dublin   1968

Oil on canvas   5 ¼ x 4 ft.

Nationalgalerie, acquired 1983 with proceeds from the German Lottery, Berlin

On October 11, 1963, an art happening was announced in Düsseldorf: "Leben mit Pop" (Life with Pop). In Berges, a furniture store, a sofa, table, chairs, armchair, and television stood on pedestals, proclaimed as works of art. Two men in suits acted as living sculptures: Gerhard Richter and Konrad Lueg. They had planned this "Demonstration for Capitalist Realism" together with Sigmar Polke und Manfred Kuttner. This term was meant to be understood as an amusingly ironical counter-offensive to the pathetically devotional doctrine of "Socialist Realism" on the other side of the Wall. The term "German Pop" was also mentioned.

Born in Lower Silesia in 1941, Sigmar Polke emigrated with his parents to West Germany when he was twelve and began his training as a glass painter. Like Gerhard Richter, while studying at the Düsseldorf Kunstakademie he attended the classes of the Art Informel painter Karl Otto Goetz. The happening mentioned above was, in view of the abstractions of Art Informel, Tachisme, and Zero, the first programmatic manifestation of the new concept of art in the Federal Republic and corresponded to other social ideas. The effects are visible to this day. The artistically influential milieu in Düsseldorf was formulated by Joseph Beuys, whose open concept of art probably confirmed Polke in his composition of images as well as in his intuitive actions. Polke and Richter, who were friends, discovered the trivial as an artistic medium. In this, they were inspired by American Pop Art although they developed their own forms. Polke's approach was highly complex from the start. His vast oeuvre is proof of his sensational creative talent.

Polke works from photographs. He not only copies the trivial motifs, but also reproduces the halftone effect of magazine and newspaper illustrations dot for dot. This is a painstaking process demanding endless patience. Later, he also worked with

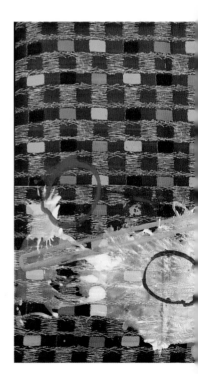

various stencils. From 1963 to the present day, he has used this technique which he has continually refined by many variations. Over the years, the dots have become a trademark for his work. As Polke explained in an interview in 1966: "For me, the halftone technique is a system…. It takes apart, scatters, puts in order, and makes everything equal…. In this regard, I believe that my 'halftone' way of seeing … is a universal interpretation."

The picture *Dublin* dates from 1968. The photographic, trivial motif could be a view of any town; the process employed has distilled it out of abstraction. The illustration nears the realm of the imaginary, dissolved into the sum of its parts which actually prove to be constituent elements. With this method, Polke investigates the essence of painting.

Another facet of Polke's work is represented by the so-called "Stoffbilder" (fabric pictures). These are works in which already available, mostly patterned fabrics (curtain and upholstery fabric, felt, suit fabric, tiger-print, etc.) serve as the picture surface to be painted. These textiles chosen by Polke were another way in which the artist upset popular expectations of art.

Manöverschaden from 1986, painted on red checked fabric, stimulated Polke to a new way of creating dynamic images. The ordering, screen-like weave of the fabric creates interaction with the smudged and washed-out painting. The foreground and background are woven together by the almost tachiste blots of paint.   *B.S.*

Sigmar Polke   born 1941
lives in Cologne

Manöverschaden (Damage from Maneuvers)   1986

Emulsion paint on furnishing fabric
6 ³/₄ x 12 ¹/₂ ft.

Nationalgalerie, acquired 1994 with proceeds from the German Lottery, Berlin

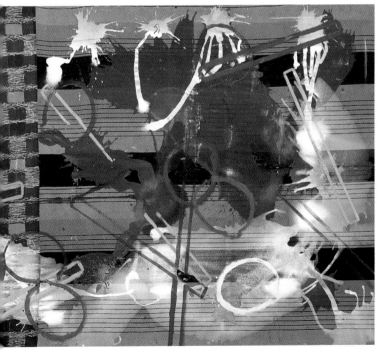

Georg Baselitz born 1938
lives in Holle

Ciao America   1988–89
Color woodcut   5 ³/₄ x 4 ¹/₂ ft.

Kupferstichkabinett, acquired 1989 with aid from the
Artists' Sponsorship Fund of the Senate's Office for
Science, Research, and Cultural Affairs, Berlin

Born as Georg Kern in 1938 in the town of Deutschbaselitz in Saxony, Georg Baselitz moved to West Berlin at the end of the 1950s. His "Heldenbilder" (Pictures of Heroes) contain everything that contradicted the triumphant march of the American avant-garde and the Art Informel movement at that time, from their coloration to their brushwork to their "heroes" theme. But Baselitz's blunt declaration of faith in representational art was also not in line with the trends in painting in the early years of the GDR. He distances the motifs from the viewer in his pictures, confirming their "unimportance" in his written commentaries. He has expressed this distancing in a radical manner since 1969. In that year of crisis in the Federal Republic, he turned his motifs around and stood them on their heads. In this way he forces the viewer to differentiate more exactly between factual and expressive reality, and preserves aesthetic scope for the subject-orientated contingency of his creation.

The large woodcut *Ciao America*, executed 1988–89 in three colors, pays homage to the Berlin gallery owner, Rudolf Springer. In 1966, along with Michael Werner, Springer had exhibited Baselitz's largest "Heldenbild," *The Great Friends*. The artist described his work: "They are birds, but because they are upside-down and consist only of lines and the splinters of light colors flashing through the dark surface, it is difficult to recognize them as birds and know how many there are of them." The number of the animals in the picture is related to the 40th anniversary of the gallery. Three white birds are particularly noticeable. Baselitz explains further: "These three are singled out as something like the crank on a pepper-mill, or the dinghy hanging behind a trawler and dancing on the waves." These words illustrate a compositional problem unique to the pictures of the 1980s and early 1990s. "Just like a fly on the edge of a plate, the first bird was supposed to be cut randomly into the wood, preferably in the place least expected, so that the remaining thirty-nine could gather around as if by chance."

Bildsieben, dated 1991, deals with this problem of center and periphery. The middle of the large and unusually light canvas of radiant colors seems to have been blotted out. A black area with two skulls denies access into the picture. Thematically, these skulls are a reminder of Adam's grave which, according to legend,

Georg Baselitz born 1938
lives in Holle

Torso 1993
Linden wood, resin 61 x 30 ¹/₄ x 31 in.
The Marx Collection

was situated under Christ's cross and
is present in all Renaissance crucifixion scenes. Subordination and
coordination, representation and
abstraction; the poles of pictorial
possibilities in *Bildsieben* are offset
against each other. Pure — that is,
abstract — painting seems to have
crept in here over the corpse of
figurative art.

Baselitz's sculptural work began,
just as his painting, with a scandal.
The block-like figure with the ambig-
uously raised right arm (today in The
Ludwig Collection, Cologne) caused
protest. His *Torso* from 1991 is also
contradictory and frightening. The
body has been hewn out of a tree
trunk with rough blows. The breasts
and pudenda have been painted red.
Here, the process required for the
work's making are also clear: the
search for form and the resistance of
the material. "Transformation is also
always an act of violence." The
artist's words are given immediate
visual form.   *I.W.D.*

Georg Baselitz born 1938
lives in Holle

Bildsieben (Picture Seven) 1991
Oil on canvas 9 ¹/₄ x 15 ft.
The Marx Collection

A.R. Penck   born 1939
lives in London and Berlin

Die Zukunft des Emigranten
(The Future of the Emigrant)   1983
Synthetic resin on canvas
8 $\frac{1}{2}$ x 11 $\frac{1}{2}$ ft.

Nationalgalerie, acquired 1984 by the Verein der
Freunde der Nationalgalerie

Born as Rolf Winkler, the artist has
called himself A.R. Penck since
1966. He has also been known as
"Mike Hammer", "Y," and "T.M.",
and his continual testing of new
methods of working is reflected by
these changing identities in his artistic existence.

Born in Dresden in 1939, he was
expatriated from the former GDR in
1980. His paintings were exhibited
for the first time in Dresden in 1956.
In 1961–62 he produced his first
"Weltbild" (world image) which was,
at the same time, his first "System-
bild" (system image). This was a
composition of stick figures, which
were to become a trademark in all
his subsequent work. He took this
"result of abstraction, reduction,
and logic" to be a form of realism
because "it still referred to the figure,
the human image, to events and pro-

cesses connected to mankind."

Penck included the results of his
involvement with scientific problems, especially cybernetics and
information theory, in his works.
Between 1968 and 1973, he developed the "Standart" pictures. The
name is a combination of the two
words "standard" and "art." His aim
was to work out the vocabulary for a
new, pictorial language, suitable to
the times. The pages taken from the
artist's book date from this phase and
give a visual example of Penck's conceptual approach.

As a painter, a sculptor, a draftsman, a creator of objects and books,
etchings and lithographs, a poet, and
finally a musician and teacher, Penck
has always tested himself and his art
in new contexts. The multi-dimen-
sional quality of his work has few
parallels — comparison could be
made with the early Dieter Roth and
the entire development of the Fluxus
movement. Penck's books describe
his world view in a language that
always leads straight to the heart of
the matter. It is precisely this that
shows a considerable quality of this
art system. Penck introduced the
East-West debate, which is his very

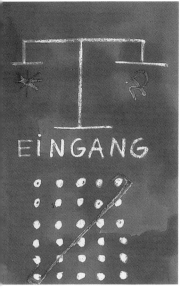

A.R. Penck born 1939
lives in London and Berlin

Standart Series No. 1, No. 11, and
No. 12 1968–73

Ink, oil crayons each 11 $\frac{1}{2}$ x 8 in.
Kupferstichkabinett, acquired 1980

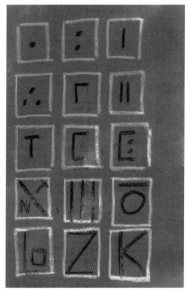

own perception of the state of the world, into the imagery of art. He translated the situation of his own life into a unique visual language. In the large picture *Die Zukunft des Emigranten*, the complicated sign language covers the canvas like a many-layered network, connecting individual gestures and behavior into a system of signals which denies any attempt to standardize the gesticulations and symbols. This picture was created four years after Penck's departure from the GDR, after he had found his first home in the West near Cologne. In 1983, he moved to London, and that explains the question about the future of the emigrant, who has trouble communicating in his new surroundings. The painting depicts a period of reflection on the way things stand, showing the path to new theories and new possibilities for imagery. *B.S.*

Anselm Kiefer   born 1945
lives in Barjac

Ohne Titel (Untitled)   1983
Emulsion, oil, shellack, woodcut,
synthetic resin, straw on canvas
8 $\frac{1}{2}$ x 6 $\frac{1}{4}$ ft.

The Marx Collection

It was neither the purely intellectual,
nor the unconscious elements in art,
but rather the world of objects and
history that first had a formative influence on Anselm Kiefer. And so his
autobiography from 1978 reads like
a young man's cataractous tour
through beautiful and dangerous areas of the past as well as the present,
finally ending with Beuys: "Motor-
bikes, marble, Jean Genet, Huys-
mans, Ludwig II of Bavaria, Paestum,
Adolf Hitler, Juliet, pictures: heroic
landscapes; 1970 own books on
heroic symbols, occupations, shots,
state examinations, study foundation
of the German people, studies with
Joseph Beuys, Düsseldorf."

It is mostly German history that
ends in catastrophe with Kiefer.
According to Bazon Brock, Kiefer

presents the German fate
of desiring greatness and
producing destruction. This
is true also in the architectural image *Ohne Titel*. The
overpowering emptiness of
fascist architecture is de-
nounced by its own enor-
mity as an empty shell for
the lifeless and inhumane.
A painter's tiny palette
hanging high in space
takes up the theme of "Bil-
derstreit" (feud of images)
that Kiefer once staged in
his atelier with three toy
tanks around a broken palette. The artist is constantly
concerned about the political power to promote cer-
tain images and forbid others. In this feud between
images, Kiefer always sides
with the forbidden ones.

Only if these generally
forbidden images of fascist art and
architecture — so devoid of good
taste and decency — are ruthlessly
pointed out, can we break their spell
of pathos and the power to blind.
According to Kiefer, the showing of
forbidden images, which demonstate
so cerimoniously the unspeakable
errings in German art history and
philosophy, gives us just the opportunity we need to liberate ourselves
from them.

In *Cherubim-Seraphim*, also from
1983, the pathos is directed at a
Judeo-Christian context. Two great,
shining white boulders lying in a
field have the Old-Testament names
for angels written above them. A particular feud concerning what images
may or may not do was also sparked
off by the way angels were represented. Already in the early Middle Ages
they were presented in human form
without any justification from biblical sources. Wings enabled them to
hover in space. Kiefer destroys the
theme's pictorial tradition and en-
cumbers the companions of God
with considerable worldly weight.

In this roundabout manner he comes back to the forbidding of false images in the Ten Commandments. Jews are forbidden to make an image of the teachings of God. One way of getting around this is to give things new associations as here, where stones in a field represent angels.

Making distress visible as a prerequisite for dissent is also the artistic principle behind Kiefer's *Volkszählung* from 1991. The work is also known as *60 Million Peas*. Kiefer expressed anger at the power of the state by evoking the senseless activity of counting peas as a metaphor for the census, which reduces citizens to peas. State surveillance, against which Kiefer is protesting here by recalling his boycott of the 1988 census, of course has roots reaching back to biblical times and the census at Christ's birth.

Turning from pictures to objects made in his preferred material, lead, Kiefer widens his vision from the history of the Germans to the history of mankind. The decisive impulse was given by his study of the thoughts of Jewish intellectuals driven from Hitler's Germany. So Benjamin's "angel of history," who looks back at paradise but always also surveys the ruins of history, appears in Kiefer's lead aircraft *Mohn und Gedächtnis*, a reference to the metaphors in Paul Celan's collection of poetry *Mohn und Gedächtnis*. Poppies, as a symbol of intoxication and dreams, lie between the pages of books. Books represent for Kiefer the archives of remembrance. A wealth of pictorial themes such as "Wege der Weltweisheit" (The Ways of Worldly Wisdom), or "Hoffmann von Fallersleben auf Helgoland" (Hoffmann of Fallersleben in Helgoland) were first put into book form by Kiefer and catalogued, later to be used to create images and finally construct objects in lead. The books on the wings of the aircraft are a symbol for Kiefer of the visible par-

Anselm Kiefer   born 1945
lives in Barjac

Cherubim-Seraphim   1983
Mixed technique on canvas
9 1/4 x 11 ft.

Nationalgalerie, acquired 1984 by the Verein der Freunde der Nationalgalerie

Anselm Kiefer   born 1945
lives in Barjac

Mohn und Gedächtnis (Poppy and
Memory)   1989
Lead, glass, poppies, iron
7 $^1/_2$ x 21 $^1/_4$ x 20 $^1/_2$ ft.
The Marx Collection

adox when the intellectual business
of art counteracts the weight of the
material and its disintegration. This
struggle for artistic deliverance from
that which is earthly and temporal,
symbolized by the aircraft, is emphasized visually by Kiefer through the
frequent use of lead as the material
for his objects. Long associated with
the planet Saturn owing to its weight
and gray-black color, lead is also the
raw material of the alchemical process by which gold is won from base
materials by cleaning and refining. In
the use of lead as the preferred material for his objects and the almost ex-
clusive choice as a ground for his
paintings (as in his many variations
on Dürer's engraving *Melencolia*),
Kiefer reveals his entire body of work
as "Saturnian art." Its themes under
the sign of Saturn, the planet of disaster, are the catastrophes of history:
war, destruction, and death. Kiefer's
favorite colors for representing such
catastrophes are black and gray, the
colors of Saturn and of the melan-

choly that planet induces. Earth, straw, ashes, and lead: these materials attributed to Saturn are Kiefer's preferred media.

By provoking the viewer with taboo images, by using feuding images as a protest against every censure of pictures, and by stimulating the viewer through an awareness of spaces blocked out or left empty to conceptions outside the bounds of vision, Kiefer allows him to participate in the creative act of art. According to the Neoplatonic-cabalistic tradition that Kiefer absorbed through the writings of Benjamin, this creative act aspires to overcome all things earthly and ends in the ascent to higher spheres. No one manages this ascent better than the melancholic individual who, through learning and melancholic sensation, through *Mohn und Gedächtnis*, reconciles this fragmented creation with its creator. *P.K.S.*

Anselm Kiefer   born 1945
lives in Barjac

Volkszählung (Census)   1991
Steel, lead, peas, photographs
13 $^1/_2$ x 18 $^3/_4$ x 26 $^1/_4$ ft.
The Marx Collection, owned by the state of Berlin

Blinky Palermo
(Peter Heisterkamp) 1943–77

4 Prototypen (4 Prototypes) 1970
Color silk screens
each 23 $^1/_2$ x 23 $^1/_2$ in.

Kupferstichkabinett, acquired 1981

Blinky Palermo categorized his
works into wall painting, drawing,
fabric pictures, and print making.
Among these, the latter is entitled to
represent the complete works, as it is
"like all of his other groups of works.
Without replacing, copying, imitat-
ing, reproducing any of them, this is
the group that most clearly stands
for the others: pars pro toto"
(J. Cladders, 1983).

Within this group, the 4 Prototypen require special attention on the
grounds of their title and their frequent repetition in different arrangements. The components of this fixed
grouping are an equilateral triangle,
an asymmetrical triangle, a square,

and an almost oval-shaped disc.
Their combination is characterized
by correspondence and ambivalence. The two centered, hieratic figures on the left are placed opposite
an organic and a dynamic form on
the right, which doubles their inter-
play since both horizontal and diagonal visual links are the result. The
fine-tuned quality of their relationship is echoed in the subdued colors
with their measured shifts in tone
and, counter to the ideals of Concrete and Minimal Art, in the impre-
cision of the contours, which are
lively due to their slight deviations
from geometric norms.   A.D.

C.O. Paeffgen born 1933
lives in Cologne

Rosa Mond (Pink Moon), R.N.4596
1982
PUR foam rubber
35 $^1/_2$ x 24 $^3/_4$ x 6 in.
Nationalgalerie, acquired 1983

A large, fully rounded, pink moon.
This work of C.O. Paeffgen looks like
child's play. Its material, its hand-
smoothed surface, and its emphati-
cally voluminous form give this impression. The synthetic effect of the
color is reminiscent of ice cream.

The original form is not the point
of departure for Paeffgen's pictorial
work, but the publicly effective image capable of fostering consensus.
Stereotypes can often be found in
his painting. The monumentally enlarged press photographs, portraits,
and self-portraits are taken from posters, newspapers, and magazines.
The artist seizes upon these images
from the daily business of visual
communication and paints a broad
black contour around them. When
they reappear in Paeffgen's art, they
look like comic strips, like stencils or
patterns of a visual convention. Paeffgen is not interested in the model
and the ideal in an aesthetic sense,
but in a sense of enlightenment. How
do images function, how do they
stimulate us, and what do they communicate?

Returning to the moon, one thing
becomes evident in this playing
around with social patterns of perception: how far we have distanced
ourselves from reality. Our ciphers
and symbols do not permit the moon
to have its own physical form, nor its
own color or shape. Paeffgen's moon
is a cliché of a cliché. In its plump
form, the moon hands its appearance
back to us: we see ourselves.

I.W.D.

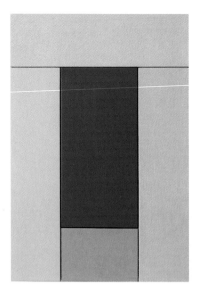

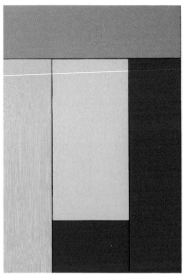

Imi Knoebel born 1940
lives in Düsseldorf

2 Porträts (2 Portraits): Agnes, Heidi
1995

Acrylic on panel
each 19 ³/₄ x 13 ³/₄ in.

Nationalgalerie, acquired 1996 with the aid of the
Preussischer Kulturbesitz and proceeds from the
German Lottery, Berlin

Together with Imi (Rainer) Giese
(1942–1974), Imi (Wolfgang) Knoebel went from the Werkkunstschule,
Darmstadt to the Düsseldorf Kunstakademie in 1964. Both of them
were drawn there by Joseph Beuys,
although he had no formal influence
on Knoebel as a teacher. The installation in room 19 of the Düsseldorf
Kunstakademie has become a legend
among the work of the two "Imis."
By arranging the simplest of shapes
made out of hardboard throughout
the whole room, they caused a small
sensation. Such uncompromising,
"minimalist" reductions were still
unusual at that time. All students
recognized a kind of ground zero in
this provoking, reduced installation
and saw how far the two had distanced themselves from their teacher,
Beuys. By using elementary forms in
their work, they asked fundamental
questions about painting and sculp-

ture. In the series "Konstellationen"
(Constellations), Knoebel formulated
the problem of combining and fusing
together simple rectangles. He tries

out all possibilities in these series in order to find the valid answer to the question about the valid image. Their respective design is his argument. By giving each constellation its own title, he permits representational associations. For *Konstellation S. Cadmiumrot*, the material itself is the subject matter.

The more recent series of "12 Porträts" (12 Portraits) consists of small pictures, identical in size and format, made up of colored panels and strips. The titles are female Christian names which are placed in a fixed sequence. The pictures are built up of cleverly chosen and extraordinarily beautiful colors whose brushstrokes are barely perceptible. Indeed, in the few places where they almost accidentally shine through, they give the picture an unmistakable focal point. Each one of these pictures possesses its own character; their similarities bring out their dis-

similarities. Names permit associations, and a curious thread is spun between the abstract image and the trivial associations suggested by familiar first names.

The central colored field, which appears to be framed by the other fields around it, generally determines the character and at the same time pushes the viewer back with the purity of its expanse — like an icon, like a vision, detached from the category of picture or sculpture.   *B.S.*

Imi Knoebel   born 1940
lives in Düsseldorf

Konstellation S. Cadmiumrot
(Constellation S. Cadmium Red)
1975–85

Oil on plywood   8 $^1/_2$ x 13 $^1/_4$ ft.
Nationalgalerie, acquired 1985

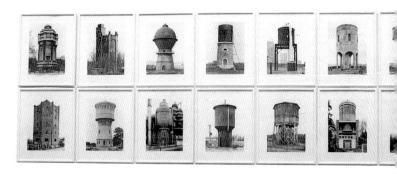

Bernd and Hilla Becher

born 1931 and 1934
live in Düsseldorf

Wassertürme (Water Towers)
1967–84

20 Photographs
each 15 $^3/_4$ x 11 $^3/_4$ in.

Nationalgalerie, acquired 1985

Bernd and Hilla Becher have worked together as photographers since the late 1950s. Until 1965, they mainly photographed the half-timbered houses of the Siegerland, the industrial areas in the Ruhr, and in Holland. Objects dating from the earliest period of industrialization — silos, water towers, blast furnaces, pit-head towers, large machinery, and buildings — were recorded for their technical appearance. By now this work contains examples from every continent which has been home to technological and industrial developments. These image series put forward typologies of functional buildings, comparisons of encyclopedic value, or even conclusions. An "unintentional aesthetic" (Becher) results. The subject matter of the pictures is presentbeuysed in a distant, almost epic manner. The serial approach corresponds to the theories of Conceptual Art as developed in the 1960s. However, the works still have a narrative quality grounded in the subject matter itself. Starting with groupings dictated by the subjects' function, the images are next ordered according to their building materials, thus forming families of objects. The technical precision of the camera is used to its full advantage and all objects are given the same emphasis. No differences and no appraisals are made between things; no assertions are put forward.

The buildings of the *Wassertürme* tableau are shown, as in nearly all the studies of different types of building, in strict frontality. Only a few examples of water towers have been selected — those whose basic form best illustrates the type "water tower." The viewer can read the pictures in this arrangement horizontally as well as vertically or diagonally. The richness of forms is surprising; we can see that each water tower has its individual shape and also that curious designs were invented in the drive for technical innovation. In their over thirty years of activity, the Bechers have changed our view of the industrial environment and, in general, our vision of objects. Similarities and dissimilarities heighten our amazement of everyday objects.

Based on a comprehensive understanding of their subjects, a knowledge of their diverse representations and their functional interrelationships, Bernd and Hilla Becher have developed a system of images bearing their unmistakable hallmark.

B.S.

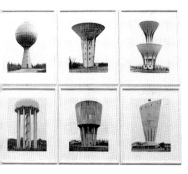

Hanne Darboven   born 1941
lives in Hamburg

Milieu 80 Posthum (Posthumous
Milieu 80)   1987

Ink, collage on paper
56 pages   each 16 1/2 x 11 3/4 in.

Nationalgalerie, acquired 1988 by the Verein der
Freunde der Nationalgalerie

The works of the conceptual artist
Hanne Darboven, often seem austere
and economical. But on closer examination, we recognize a point of
departure and a point of reference for
thoughts that go much further —
thoughts that have to do with the existence of mankind. She
is concerned with the
thought processes in-
volved in recording and
assimilating dimensions
of time. Darboven has
developed a method by
which periods of time
are transferred into a
new system of measur-
ing units according to a
special index. Thus re-
corded, the time is then
translated by mathemat-
ical calculations into
new constructions of
symbols and numbers.
In the work *Milieu 80
Posthum*, these reflec-
tions are shown in the
top left-hand third of
each of the written
pages. Already this pro-
cess of abstraction, a
visual representation of
one year of life, demonstrates the in-
comprehensibility of passing time
and how unfathomable it is to attempt to represent it. This method of
exaggeration and almost compulsive
systematization enables a visualiza-
tion of the abstract expression "time"
through continuous recording. The
viewer is continually reminded of the
real length of time involved in the
work of art, something that he can
not see and so must imagine. On the
page, next to the numbers, Hanne
Darboven writes two columns in her
even handwriting and adds three
photographs from her studio. We see
the worktables in a room full of objects, many handwritten books, and
thousands of handwritten pages that
represent an entire living cosmos.

The clarity of the work's structure
and the diversity produced by the
rhythm of the passing year join together incomprehensibly in a special
way.   *B.S.*

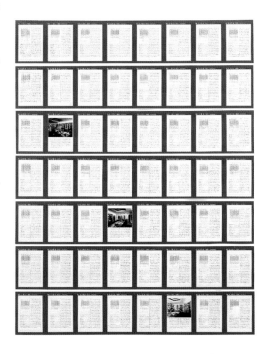

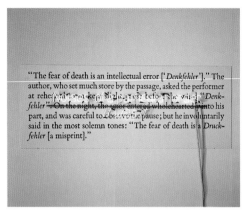

"The fear of death is an intellectual error ['*Denkfehler*']." The author, who set much store by the passage, asked the performer at rehearsal to make a slight pause before the word "*Denkfehler*." On the night, the actor entered wholeheartedly into his part, and was careful to observe the pause; but he involuntarily said in the most solemn tones: "The fear of death is a *Druckfehler* [a misprint]."

an intellectual level. The relationship of the viewer to the statement that fear of death is an error in thinking is provoked by the text. The significance of that relationship is on an intellectual-sensory plane which exists as its context outside of the work. The meaning is formed individually by each viewer in an active, critical assessment; with this process the work is completed.   *M.M.*

Joseph Kosuth   born 1945
lives in Ghent and New York

It Was It No. 5   1986

Text photograph, applied neon writing
2 $^1/_2$ x 7 ft.

Nationalgalerie, acquired 1988

Joseph Kosuth published his book *Art after Philosophy* in 1969. It formulates wide-reaching tendencies for the theoretic self-perception of the analytical currents in Conceptual Art. Kosuth sees art as an idea. The relationship between word and image is of medial significance to his understanding of art. The viewer is introduced to a combination of word, image, and light, whose meaning can only be deduced from the interaction of all elements. The content of the work is based on these elements but is more than the mere sum of those parts. In the 1980s, Kosuth extended his earlier model "Kunst/Sprache" (art/language) with the category of "Kontext" (context). The text excerpts, such as the quotation from Freud's *Psychopathology of Everyday Life* (1901), used by Kosuth in *It Was It*, confront the viewer on

Reiner Ruthenbeck   born 1937
lives in Ratingen

Stoffbahn mit Glasplatte II
(Width of Cloth with Plate of Glass)
1970–85

Glass, cloth   8 $^1/_2$ x 4 $^1/_2$ x 3 $^1/_4$ ft.

Nationalgalerie, acquired 1985

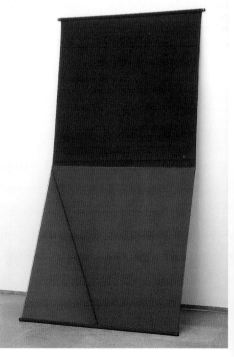

Reiner Ruthenbeck says he wants to instill his works with peace. In objects such as *Stoffbahn mit Glasplatte*, the unpretentious material, freed from any associations of function, is combined with a minimalist, intellectual severity. In doing so, Ruthenbeck refers indirectly to Arte Povera as well as to Conceptual Art. Despite this, his works, which articulate and alter the space surrounding them, are of a meditative character. In *Stoffbahn mit Glasplatte*, the diversity of materials employed establishes the effect and hermetic quality of the work. It is only through the different transparencies, thicknesses, and weights of the separate elements that this production develops its meaning. Together, the canvas treated with textile paint and the plate of glass appear as a three-dimensional object in a manner appropriate to a statue. Their form, color, and materiality come alive as they enter into relationships with the wall, the floor, light, and shadow. The intellectual approach and philosophical assumption behind the work do not aim to unite contrasting elements, but to visibly remove contradictions in the material.　　*J.M.*

Erwin Heerich　　born 1922
lives in Meerbusch

Kartonplastiken (Sculptures in Cardboard)　1968–80
Cardboard
each 15 $^1/_4$ x 15 $^1/_4$ x 15 $^1/_4$ in.
Nationalgalerie, acquired 1985

Erwin Heerich studied, as Beuys did, with Ewald Mataré at the Düsseldorf Kunstakademie. His works are a prime example of a rational and analytical approach to art. Since the 1960s, the artist's imagined world, in which new definitions of surface and building elements are created, has been expressed in drawings and geometric structures on cardboard. The symbolism contained in the eternal forms of his *Kartonplastiken* contrasts with the lightness and makeshift, "poor" character of the brown cardboard, whose only function is to clarify the ordered scheme of the construction. Here, improvisation has been replaced by the attempt to let the viewer experience sculpture and architectural form as the results of mathematical law.　　*M.M.*

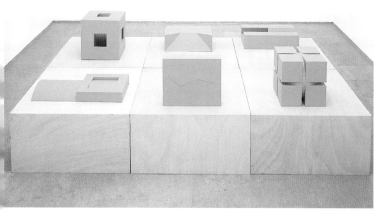

Franz Erhard Walther   born 1939
lives in Hamburg

Großes Stoffbuch (Great Fabric Book)
1969
68 pages, coarse cotton fabric
6 ³/₄ x 4 x ³/₄ ft.
Nationalgalerie, acquired 1980

Franz Erhard Walther has been working on the concept for his fabric
books since 1963. They are made of
heavy cotton material with sewn-on
covers of hardboard. The Nationalgalerie also acquired drawings,
sketches, and photographs from the
artist which document and explain
his approach to the exhibited work.
For Walther, the usability of his objects is more important than their
material presence. He has continually pointed out the broadening of his
artistic concept, and has extended
Hegel's definition of art as a "material manifestation of an idea" to include the aspect of practical applica-
tions. Expressions used by him to
describe his works include "Hand-
lung" (action), "Handlungsprozeß"
(process of action), and "Benutzbar-
keit" (usability).

The *Große Stoffbuch* lies on the
floor. Each page defines actions for
up to four users. It has pockets, tucks,
and loops which instruct the viewer
to stand on the book or to lie down

in it. The aim of Walther's concept is
the interaction of object and user.
"The user has the responsibility for
the work" is one of the key statements of his approach to art.

Owing to the user's active involvement with the work, the commensu-
rablity of proportions is important
to the artist. The size, form and, not
least, the material, the coarse cotton
fabric, create a feeling for one's own
body and the space surrounding it. In
an elevated sense, Walther's works
are architecture. They follow the tradition of Leonardo's studies of proportion and Le Corbusier's Modulor.

The concept of the fabric sculptures is not aimed at meditation.
Walther wants to evoke a state, an
at-peace-with-oneself, a standing-in-
oneself, a being-with-oneself, and,
as he says himself, to bring about a
"peaceful" situation. The viewer is
invited to take part in an active way
and the concrete action opposes the
romantic understanding of art.   *I.W.D.*

Franz Erhard Walther born 1939
lives in Hamburg

Zeitkörper (Bodies of Time)
1967–72
Page 1: pencil, watercolor, oil;
Page 2: pencil, watercolor, ballpoint
pen, ink, oil   11 ¹/₂ x 8 ¹/₄ in.
Kupferstichkabinett, acquired 1987 as a gift from the
artist

With his fifty-eight-piece "1. Werksatz" (1st Work Group) from 1963 to
1969, Walther created a new type of
sculpture. For his works in fabric are
not autonomous "finished" constructions, relating to a viewer. Rather,
they attain their inherent form
through the user, providing him with
instruments with which space, time,
and volume may be experienced.
The drawing *Zeitkörper* belonging
to "Kopf Leib Glieder" (Head Body
Limbs) from the "1. Werksatz" demonstrates on one side an exemplary
posture used in handling the object
and on the other, the alternating
positions of the five participants.

Rotschrift was produced analo-
gously in conjunction with the sculptural series "Wandformationen"
(Wall Formations), which is based
on human dimensions. This work on
paper is laid out in a more pictorial

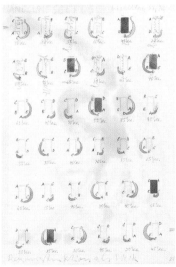

way, though, quite capable of standing on its own. It differs from nearly
all the other drawings of the "1. Werksatz" in that it is only drawn on one
side of the paper.   *A.D.*

Franz Erhard Walther born 1939
lives in Hamburg

Rotschrift (Red Script)   1978–81
Pencil, opaque water paints
11 ¹/₂ x 8 ¹/₄ in.
Kupfestichkabinett, acquired 1988

Klaus Rinke born 1939
lives in Haan

Mutation 1970
112 Photographs
each 23 1/4 x 17 in.
Nationalgalerie, acquired 1979

In 1970, Klaus Rinke, assisted by the photographer Monika Baumgartl, began producing series of photographs with the human body as a subject. The title "Mutation" is misleading, for all photographs show self-portraits of the artist who, in a strictly systematic way, records the variety of gestures of his arms, hands, and fingers as body positions. They hide the portrait, showing only part of the visage — but never the whole, open face. The viewer finds himself in front of 112 variations of one figure. Every one of the postures is believable. They can be experienced as a time dimension. They show sequences of movements, some of which follow directly after the other and others that change more abruptly. The artist as a medium of himself? There is no personal "hallmark" functioning as communicator and bearer of artistic identity. The theme is that the photographic reproduction itself is to be considered as the work. The only sense of design is contained in the gestures and the principle behind the serial layout. The language of the body is documented completely without vanity. An apparent reduction of artistic means to include only the physical persona of the artist results in a clear exhibition of psychic moments. These give the work an existential dimension which, in turn, emerges from this throw-back onto the self. The concealment of the face by one's own body has a distancing effect and creates alienation despite all intimacy and authenticity. The series documents a procedure close to Process Art. Rinke calls his photographic series and the drawings which make up this group of work "primary demonstrations." They complement a facet of his production in which, from 1967 to 1984, Rinke dedicated himself to happening-type work: body-works, performances, film and video art. Just like for Beuys or Walther, it is also an artistic objective for Rinke to call attention to the diversity and richness of human creativity. His "primary dem-

onstrations" describe the basis of any action: body sensation, movement, feeling for time and space. At the same time they allow for a meditative moment that is vital for the discovery of details that cause the mutation of something well-known into something alien. The "Primary demonstrations" describe the "gestures of the body as an immaterial medium of art" (K. Thomas, 1994). In this sense, Rinke also meant "primary" in view of a "relationship to the minimalist approach to art, the 'primary structures,' while 'demonstration' addresses the vitality of the character. 'Primary demonstration' is, therefore, a living minimalist sculpture" (H.-W. Schmidt, 1992).

The order in which the portraits were arranged was originally a fixed sequence; later they were rearranged and finally displayed in varying ways. This enables the series to become a continuum without beginning or end, whose presentation and reception maintain the quality of a process. *J.M.*

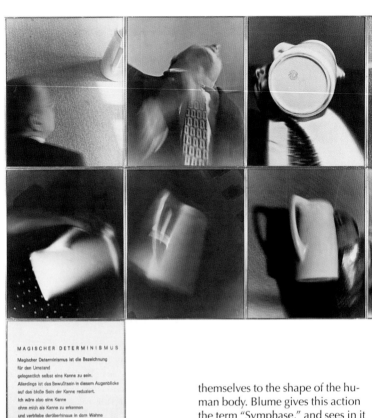

MAGISCHER DETERMINISMUS

Magischer Determinismus ist die Bezeichnung
für den Umstand
gelegentlich selbst eine Kanne zu sein.
Allerdings ist das Bewußtsein in diesem Augenblicke
auf das bloße Sein der Kanne reduziert.
Ich wäre also eine Kanne
ohne mich als Kanne zu erkennen
und verbliebe darüberhinaus in dem Wahne
im Unterschiede zu der Kanne
weiterhin ich selbst zu sein.
Dem ist aber nicht so!

Bernhard Johannes Blume

born 1937   lives in Cologne

Magischer Determinismus (Magical
Determinism)   1976

111 photographs
each 19 3/4 x 23 1/2 in.

Nationalgalerie, acquired 1985

The photographic work of Bernhard
Johannes Blume rapidly undermines
our familiar patterns of perception.
The spatial and intellectual narrow-
ness of post-war, lower middle-class
interiors serve as a foil for a revolution of things. Everyday objects like
porcelain coffee pots seem to come
to life. There is a confrontation between the objects and the subjects in
which the former attempt to mould

themselves to the shape of the human body. Blume gives this action
the term "Symphase," and sees in it
a visual representation of the philosophical question posed by German
Idealism: is man capable of perceiving things facing him, or does he
create them himself in his consciousness? A teacher of art and philosophy
for many years, to whom Beuys had
recommended a school-teaching
career in the 1960s, Blume takes a
"poetically parodying" approach to
this problem, presenting his experimental test-series in the medium of
authentic-looking amateur photos.
What looks like a spiritualist gather-
ing is, in fact, a careful balance of
surfaces, gray tones, and degrees of
focus. The inclusion of text indicates
that this work dates from the 1970s.
Since 1980, Bernhard and Anna
Blume, a husband-and-wife artist
team, have relied solely on the effect
of their images.   *D.S.*

term coined by Harald Szeemann. Whereas the choice of form is certainly individual, the longing to cross the occidental borders of rationality is the result of a collective urge — an urge defined by the hippie culture of around 1970 — which led to a romanticized view of foreign cultures.

In 1976, while on a scholarship granted by the Villa Romana in Florence, Buthe produced the large-scale *Icarus*. The figure represented is, in fact, that of the artist. In other works from the same series, Buthe also immortalized the silhouettes of his friends.

Michel de la Sainte-Beauté, as Buthe called himself in Florence, showed himself in the role of the mythical stormer of heaven, who comes too close to the sun and falls to the ground. The figure in its precarious diagonal position already seems to be enveloped in the blazing flames. By selecting this mythological reference, Buthe articulated his concern that his efforts to transform life into an enduring feast of love and beauty could not last. *D.S.*

Michael Buthe   1944–94

Icarus   1976

Mixed techniques on paper and canvas
11 ³/₄ x 9 ³/₄ ft.

Nationalgalerie, donation from the Froehlich Collection, Stuttgart, 1994

The brightly-colored cosmos of Michael Buthe is filled with impressions gained from his interest in cultures outside Europe. During numerous journeys through Africa and Asia undertaken after 1970, he took part in rituals and lived according to natural religions.

Since the exhibition of his first environment "Hommage an die Sonne" (Homage to the Sun) at the documenta 5 in Kassel (1972), Buthe's work has been referred to as "Individuelle Mythologien" (individuelle mythologies), a

Mimmo Paladino   born 1948
lives in Bologna

Senza titolo (Untitled)   1982
Oil on canvas, mixed media
6 1/2 x 9 3/4 ft.

Nationalgalerie, acquired 1984 with proceeds from the German Lottery, Berlin

The thick consistency of the deep red paint in this picture causes the foreground and background to merge into a single plane. In the center, the relief of a mask, like a fetish or death ornament, emerges from the hair of the seated woman. This ritual-like depiction can "be interpreted as a consecration or sacrifice" (Z. Felix, 1984). Mimmo Paladino explained in 1985 that he had "always made use of a representational form of painting," which was directed at "the inside of things." He shares this approach with other artists of the Italian Transavanguardia such as Chia, Clemente, and Cucchi. Against the intellectual background of postmodernism, he weaves together reality and myth, Christian symbolism and the signs of archaic or so-called primitive cultures into ornamental picture tapestries. Stimulated by Paul Klee and Max Ernst, Paladino assimilates in his works the forms used by Expressionists, by Pittura Metafisica, and Arte Povera.   *J.M.*

Sandro Chia   born 1946
lives in New York, Rome, and Florence

Genova (Genoa)   1980
Oil on canvas   7 1/2 x 13 ft.

The Marx Collection

A feature of Sandro Chia's paintings is the appearance of a clear representationalism which, however, evades a rational explanation of the significance of pictorial elements in their context. He transposes the search for the "material of the imaginary" (A.B. Oliva, 1982), which is of central importance in the painting of the Transavanguardia, particularly in the relationship between figure and space. The scenery in his painting *Genova* is reminiscent of early Mediterranean painting and of Pittura Metafisica. A dramatic, turbulent sky uniting all colors of the palette hangs over a Renaissance palace. The severe draftsmanship and precise perspective of the building and its ornamental details are surrounded on all sides by large, spontaneous sweeps of paint.

The building determines the setting. It is a self-contained whole, it guards its self-sufficiency: the architecture throws shadows onto its own walls, but not onto the square around it. In this way, the place seems to be

imaginary. This building, there "on the edge of the world," serves only itself and keeps to itself the secret of its origins and interior.

Unexpectedly, two representations of the same figure appear in front of this picture. Like the space surrounding them, they are full and baroque, and may be interpreted as representations of the self. The figures hovering above the ground express the perception of the self in the world. They describe the "feeling of space" which their "soul inhabits" (H. Geldzahler, 1986).   *J.M.*

of the head as a "small, self-contained cosmos" (E. Cucchi, 1987) has become for the painter an existential metaphor. In *Quadro Tonto*, the spiritual, mystic, tragic, and death-foreboding contents are reduced to a few elements within the picture. An oversized head — a blind mask, both embryonic and old — lays itself to rest on an imaginary-looking building. The picture tells, with all the urgency of childlike imagination, of the helplessness of man against nature — nature which plans every "becoming" and also every "passing" as inevitable fate.   *J.M.*

Enzo Cucchi   born 1950
lives in Ancona

Quadro Tonto (Stupid Picture)   1982
Oil on canvas   9 x 11 ³/₄ ft.
The Marx Collection

Enzo Cucchi's pictorial world leads us into the realms of the visionary and of legends. It is reminiscent of pantheistic cosmologies in which all of nature is subject to a higher principle. Here we do not meet man who is in possession of his environment, but rather a form of nature that predetermines the deeds of man. The representation

Bernd Koberling born 1938
lives in Berlin

Strandarbeiter (Beach Worker)
1984

Oil, synthetic resin on muslin
7 $^1/_4$ x 5 $^3/_4$ ft.

Nationalgalerie, acquired 1984 with proceeds from
the German Lottery, Berlin

After many transformations in his
work, Bernd Koberling developed an
expressive type of landscape painting. In this important sequence of
pictures, his approach is like that of a
conceptual artist in that he continu-

ally makes use of the landscape in
order to ask questions about reality.
Lava stones, cormorants, whales, and
beach workers are depicted. The picture *Strandarbeiter* dated 1984, is
one of a series on the same theme.
The figure forms the dominant,
strong vertical in the picture, while
the beam carried on his shoulder
takes up the horizon, forcing the figure into the background. The upper
body and the face of the figure
almost merge into the main yellow
field of the picture; the human is
drawn into an order imposed by ver-
ticals and horizontals. The stark contrasts in color between the blue trou-
sers and the red beam clearly divide
the motifs. *B.S.*

Karl Horst Hödicke born 1938
lives in Berlin

Sirenen (Sirens) 1982

Synthetic resin on canvas
2 parts 7 $^1/_2$ x 11 ft.

Nationalgalerie, acquired 1982 with proceeds from
the German Lottery, Berlin

The works of Karl Horst Hödicke
have played an important role in the
development of painting in Berlin.
His own peculiar blend of city motifs
and spirited painting style in large

formats was quickly received as a new style. The subjective and emotional expression in the broad brushstrokes and movement of color stood in contrast to the mainly conceptual approach to art in the 1970s. The characteristic contours and contrasting sweeps of solid color clearly relate to the painting of Expressionism.

As a teacher at the Hochschule der Künste (College of the Arts), Berlin, Hödicke encouraged and helped form the style of the artists who founded a self-help gallery at Moritz Platz and who, known as the "Moritzboys," were synonymous with the new Berlin style of painting.

Both of the figures in *Sirenen* are set into a locked dynamic in the picture: two faceless, block-like forms who use their charms to lure their victims into disaster. The contrasting directions of movement are set in broad, dark contours. The color accents in front of the gray-violet background postulate a connection arising from the strength of color and form.   *B.S.*

Rainer Fetting   born 1949
lives in Berlin

Van Gogh und Mauer V (Van Gogh and Wall V)   1978
Distemper on muslin
6 $^1/_2$ x 8 $^1/_4$ ft.
The Marx Collection

Rainer Fetting came to Berlin in 1972, attended Hans Jaenisch's class at the Hochschule der Künste, and met up with artists like Hödicke and Koberling. Even at the beginning of his career, he preferred working with large formats. In the first years, he painted portraits of friends and then Berlin, again and again, in all its big-city alienation and fascination. He began his "Van Gogh" cycle early on, of which there are two pictures in the Marx Collection. Here, we see Van Gogh captured with hasty, streaming brushstrokes on the canvas. Van Gogh is a symbolic figure of personal significance to Fetting: Van Gogh, a classic example of the lonely, misunderstood artist, is driven, nervous, and can't release his pent-up, burning tension.   *B.S.*

Robert Wilson born 1941

lives in New York

Monsters of Grace 1993

Part I: Youth, Kneeling Woman, Standing
Giant, Bench
3 wax sculptures, wooden bench, sound
installation, mixed media
Measurements vary according to
construction

Nationalgalerie, acquired 1994 with proceeds from
the German Lottery, Berlin

Robert Wilson has arranged three
figures, one behind the other, in the
space: one preparing to jump, one
kneeling, and the other lying. At first,
the figure about to jump catches our

attention as it looms above the
scene. The backrest of a wooden
bench cuts off the space at the back
of the room. The unstable pose of the
large sculpture produces a tension
that is transmitted into the space. A
movement has its starting point here
and flows into the horizontal figure,
which lies transversely to it.

Robert Wilson, who became
known in Germany through the project "Civil Wars," which traveled to
many continents, as well as through
the plays "Black Rider" and finally
"Time Rider," works with an uncon-
ventional approach to drama and
opera. His stage designs have a

change between various media and art forms.

In the static work *Monsters of Grace*, Wilson acknowledges the factor of time, which is encountered in the form of sound in the installation and makes a theatrical production out of an environment. The viewer can step between the three sculptures here and wait, so as to become part of the installation. The distance between the viewer and the stage, as found in the theater, is removed. The stage can thus be perceived as a present image. The figures, which seem to pause in contemplation, embody the "grace" mentioned in the title of the environment. Wilson himself says: "It is very important how you stand in the theater. The Japanese say that standing on the ground, the contact with the ground, is of the greatest significance for the classical theater, for the gods are under the ground, like our roots. That's why I love Marlene Dietrich so much, because she knew how to stand on the ground. She could sing three songs without having to move. She could stand."

Wilson's creations are full of surreal and mysterious moments. No prescribed contents force or determine their form. For Wilson, the unique world of art is born from the shaping of a dream as a total vision, a vision which no thought penetrates, and from which no thought escapes. This is how Johann-Karl Schmidt formulates it. He points to the hermetic quality of Wilson's art which, in its mystery and surreal nature, rejects concrete interpretation. Robert Wilson produces an intermediary art form which stimulates debate while pointing to creative paths, also outside the theater, and opening new possibilities for the museum.   K.K.

novel, dominating presence in which the spoken word has lost its ascendancy. Actions and movements on the stage are sometimes only in slow motion and have, because of this, an almost static quality. Voices and music become autonomous elements. "Language is important, the sound of language," not the meaning of the words. Wilson's theater work already makes clear that the artist disregards the hierarchies and traditional barriers of different art forms. He binds theater and performance, painting and sculpture in his creations. The viewer is meant to open himself up to a free ex-

Bernhard Leitner   born 1938
lives in Vienna

Raum-Wiege (Space Cradle)   1980
Sound-Space Object
9 $^3/_4$ x 16 x 11 $^3/_4$ ft.
Nationalgalerie, acquired 1993 by the Verein der
Freunde der Nationalgalerie

Already during the first years of his
long period in New York (1968–86),
Bernhard Leitner started work on his
idea "to structure space with sound."
Modern audio memory and control
technology allows for sounds to be
moved among their different sources,
thus producing new acoustic spatial
forms. In this sense, Leitner was the
first to use sound as a plastic material
in space. His sound-space-objects
broaden spatial experience with
auditory perception.

   In Leitner's early works, his sound
sequences are mainly linear and
acoustically curve the space or shape
it like a bowl. The basis for these
"wandering patterns of sound" are
musical tones. "In the formation of
the sounds, the basic material is so
arranged as to allow its spatially plastic character to come to the fore.
Scores are composed which precisely determine the computer-controlled timing and dynamics of the
loudspeakers' interaction. As the
sounds travel in space, crescendo

and decrescendo blend their movement from place to place into a uni-
fied motion, a line, a curve, a rocking
sensation" (H. de la Motte-Haber,
1996). The arrangement of the loudspeakers establishes a sound-space-
architecture which presents itself as
a second invisible but sensorily real
space in the given place. The external form of the *Raum-Wiege* is appropriate to its function: on entering
the sculpture, the viewer becomes a
listener for very soft, electronically
manipulated sounds describing arcs.
The material used for the sound (cel-
lo, tabla, percussion) follows the
movement of a pendulum; as the
sound moves towards the lowest
point of the arc, volume, intensity,
and tempi are increased. The fre-
quency of the sound waves is at the
same time picked up by the body
and felt as resonance. The acoustic
spatial form is perceived as a haptic
experience. Leitner defines the processes of seeing and hearing as spatial experiences and, controlled
within a defined period of time, as
experiences of being. The architecture of the *Raum-Wiege* is therefore
not an object with "sound effects." It
is far truer to say that its structure becomes the vehicle of a three-dimensional, accessible, spatial-temporal
sculpture made of sound.   *J.M.*

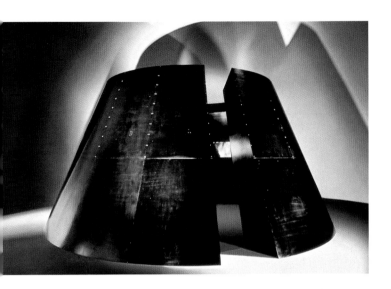

Marie-Jo Lafontaine   born 1950
lives in Brussels

Jeder Engel ist schrecklich (Every Angel Is Terrible)   1992

15 monitors, steel   10 $^1/_4$ x 22 ft.

Nationalgalerie, acquired 1993 by the Verein der Freunde der Nationalgalerie

The Antwerp-born artist became known in the 1980s above all through her environments and video sculptures. The most important works describe the rituals of power and passion in a metaphorical and associative way. They demonstrate the potential veering from beauty to danger, from sensuality and ecstasy to violence, suffering and death, from strength and discipline to powerlessness. Lafontaine remarked in 1987: "Our history is transforming itself into terror and thus accelerating its decline." The social and ecological state of the world and the experience in history that reason has been defeated time and again by the power of violence, turn the fatalism of these words into the sober truth. This is true not least for social changes that lose, pervert, or betray the "true greatness" of their ideas in reality. This contradiction between ethical demands and the real power of culture, civilization, and science is the subject matter of the video piece *Jeder Engel ist schrecklich*. Burnished steel plates, material frequently used in the armaments industry, form the stump of a cone which is almost ten feet high. Inside, fifteen color monitors are arranged in a circle. They present a repeatedly shifting montage of video clips which show blazing fires. These images are set to musical sequences by, among others, Alfred Schnittke and Arvo Pärt. The external skin of this monumental sculpture is a manifestation of the same precision which was cynically glorified in descriptions of the "Stahlgewitter" (storm of steel) during World War I. In the interior, the viewer meets the unleashed force of nature, a force of destruction. The theme relating technical perfection to destruction needs no explanation. The title of the work has its roots in the *Duino Elegies*, in which Rainer Maria Rilke describes beauty as "the terrible beginning." This touches upon an intellectual plane pointing beyond what is immediately perceptible in the sculpture's substance.

J.M.

Bruce Nauman born 1941

lives in Pecos, New Mexico

Malice   1980

Neon tubes   7 x 29 x 3 in.

The Marx Collection

Malice, a work in neon, is legible from left to right and also as a mirror image in red and green capital letters. Both words are illuminated simultaneously, producing a flickering effect. The image highlights a complex symbol of concealment and exposure, the reaction of opposing forces.

Coffee Spilled and Balloon Dog is the first work from a planned series which concerns itself with magic, sleight-of-hand, and clumsiness. In a dark room, which is intentionally bare, cold, and unfriendly, two monitors are mounted one on top of the other on a pedestal. "Coffee Spilled" can be seen in the top monitor and "Balloon Dog" below. The soundtracks for both are played simultaneously and at equally loud volumes. Here, the artist uses the extremely slow-motion technique of his early films. He picks up a full coffee cup and spills it onto the table. This is enacted so slowly that the action remains on the monitor for several minutes. The second video sequence shows a man artfully making a toy dog out of a long balloon. The movements are often imperceptible due to their slowness, and the music becomes increasingly abstract the longer the viewer stays in the room. In this work the artist goes back to elements of his artistic beginnings, when his oeuvre was characterized by the depiction of borderline experiences.

The large *Animal Pyramid* shows the skinned and reconstructed bodies of animals. Crowded tightly together, head to head, flank to flank, the naked foam bodies seem threatening

Bruce Nauman born 1941

lives in Pecos, New Mexico

Coffee Spilled and Balloon Dog   1993

2 monitors, 2 video disc recorders, 2 discs, sound
Measurements vary according to construction

The Marx Collection

Bruce Nauman   born 1941
lives in Pecos, New Mexico

Animal Pyramid   1989
Solid foam, iron, wood, wire
12 x 7 x 8 ft.
The Marx Collection

and unreal. In 1989 Nauman produced a number of animal sculptures depicting sadistic impulses and atrocities: the problems resulting from the power humans have over animals. This pyramid is one of the largest and most complex works of this series. The generalized forms of the animals are without eyes, ears, tails, hooves, or genitals. They are bound together with wire; they bump into each other, defenceless, useless, like in the slaughterhouse. Nauman commented on this body of work in 1989: "They came about through a sort of violence which had been inflicted on them, and because of this they are somehow frightening."

B.S.

like arrangement of the monitors, reminiscent of the crucifixion of Christ, suggests the artist's biography as a path of suffering. The overcoming of a difficult path becomes a martyrdom; the dive into water symbolizes death. The synchronous sound track plays back the sounds of the journey through the landscape, thus heightening the drama of the figuration. The man, stigmatized by his environment, has fallen apart hopelessly. The viewer tries in vain to reconstruct the figure which, although appearing present through its movements, has slipped away from the center.   E.B.

Gary Hill   born 1951
lives in Santa Monica

Crux   1983–87
5 channel video installation (NTSC, color, sound)
5 video monitors, 5 loudspeakers, 1 synchronizer
Nationalgalerie, acquired 1993 by the Verein der Freunde der Nationalgalerie

The central concerns of the video works by Gary Hill involve the relationship between language and images. Hill starts from sculptural expressions such as sound and body. In the work *Crux* he chooses the human body as the main theme for the first time. Hill attached five video cameras to his body in such a way that they recorded the movements of his hands, feet, and head. His wanderings begin in the ruins of a castle and end at a lake, which he dives into. We can interpret his striding through the landscape, his overcoming of obstacles, as symbolic actions, as a metaphor for human existence. Through the use of video segmentation, the imprisonment of the individual in time and space, the state of captivity in one's self, and the impossibility of perceiving oneself from outside of the self indirectly become the visual subject matter. The cross-

Peter Campus   born 1937
lives in New York

Lus   1977
Video installation   9 $^3/_4$ x 3 $^1/_4$ ft.
Nationalgalerie, acquired 1994 by the Verein der Freunde der Nationalgalerie

During his psychology studies, Peter Campus analyzed the phenomena of perception. Since then, he has tackled the same theme in his video

work. *Lus* is one of the latest large-scale video works by Peter Campus. It was shown for the first time at the documenta 6 in Kassel in 1977. When the viewer steps into the range of the camera, he sees his own oversized image projected upside down onto the screen. Campus is concerned with the sensory experiences of the viewer during the confrontation with the projected "I" in a room without light: "I walk into the field of the image again. My image and I stand vertical to one another. The image is alive. The equation between material and light energy is established. Light photons penetrate the wall. I feel the emptiness surrounding me. I give myself over to the extension of my being. For one short moment, I am at the same time this image and this self" (P. Campus, 1979). *E.B.*

Bill Viola   born 1951
lives in Long Beach

He Weeps for You   1976

Video-sound installation
Camera, projector, drum

Nationalgalerie, acquired 1993 by the Verein der Freunde der Nationalgalerie

The video installation *He Weeps for You* is one of the earliest works by Bill Viola, which brought him into the limelight for the first time at the documenta 6 in Kassel. It attempts, as do all of his visual stagings, to arouse states of consciousness which lie beyond our everyday experiences. *He Weeps for You* shows, with the aid of a video camera equipped with a special lens projecting within a closed cycle onto a screen, the image of the viewer reflected in a drop of water, which finally drips

down. Apart from this, the viewer is only aware of the sound of the drop falling on an electronically amplified drum. This procedure is repeated endlessly. The moment in which the image appears resembles the process of birth, the formation of the drop shows a lifetime, while the sound captures the moment of departure.

Over and above this, Viola tries to produce cosmic connections. "The piece makes reference to the traditional philosophy or belief that everything on the higher order of existence reflects, and is contained in, the manifestation and operation of the lower orders. This idea has been expressed in ancient religious terms as the symbolic correspondence of the mundane (the earth) and the divine (the heavens), and is also represented in theories of contemporary physics that describe how each particle of matter in space contains knowledge of or information about the entire system" (B. Viola, 1995).

Viola was twenty-six years old when he produced this seminal work. Until now, the video has only been shown in temporary exhibitions. Now in the Hamburger Bahnhof, it is part of a permanent museum display for the first time. *E.B.*

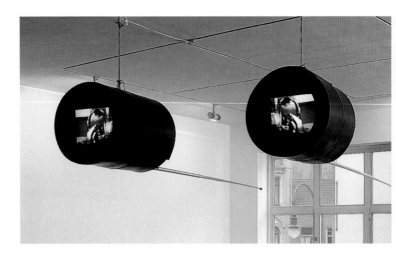

Klaus vom Bruch   born 1952
lives in Cologne

Brattain & Bardeen   1990

2 monitors, antennae, tapes

Nationalgalerie, acquired 1995 by the Verein der Freunde der Nationalgalerie

In the German video work of the late 1980s, reflections on perception are often linked to political statements. Klaus vom Bruch, with his installation *Brattain & Bardeen*, reacted to the Gulf War and the reporting done by correspondents of the American news channel CNN, which broadcasted "live" on the US air attacks on the invading Iraqi troops in Kuwait.

Clips from war footage are blended with images of the face of the artist, who thus seems to be an eyewitness. The work is dedicated to two pioneers of information technology used in warfare; the Nobel prizewinners for physics Walter H. Brattain and John Bardeen, together with William B. Shockley, invented the transistor in 1947. The semiconductor, which developed from this discovery, enabled the conventional electron tubes to be replaced by the smaller, more powerful transistors. Vom Bruch encases both monitors in black rubber cylinders, emphasizes through antennae the passive reception of the public, and allows the ghosts who called out "Brattain and Bardeen" to hover threateningly over the heads of the strolling art-gazers.

D.S.

Ulrike Rosenbach   born 1944
lives in Homburg

Or-Phelia   1987

3 video recorders, 3 monitors, 3 tapes, steel stand, and pane of glass

Nationalgalerie, acquired 1995 by the Verein der Freunde der Nationalgalerie

Three monitors lie on the floor with their screens pointing upwards. The white body of a woman appears to be drifting in a red river. An enlarged image of a human blood-stream flows through the figure, forming a connection to the life-giving source. The sound of water and flute music create a meditative mood.

The figure of Orpheus, whose singing tamed wild animals, but who was later torn apart by the Bacchantes, is linked here with Shakespeare's Ophelia, who drowned herself over an unrequited love.

Rosenbach, Beuys' "master" student, has been active in the fields of video and performance since 1972. During the 1970s, she set out in search of female role models. Happenings clearly understood as feminist art, such as her shooting of a reproduction of a Madonna (1975), made the artist well-known. As she asked at the time: "Are there any sources which give women strength to find their own essential character?"

In 1983, her search led Rosenbach to Bhagwan, and the emphasis she had put on an antagonism between the sexes was superseded by the vision of a spiritual balance of polarities. It is in this sense that Orpheus and Ophelia bond together into an androgynous *Or-Phelia*.   *D.S.*

Marcel Odenbach   born 1953
lives in Cologne

As if Memories Could Deceive Me
1984–86

3 video recorders, 3 monitors, 2 tapes
Measurements vary according to construction

Nationalgalerie, acquired 1995 by the Verein der Freunde der Nationalgalerie

The clashing of stark contrasts have been a central motif and compositional principle for Marcel Odenbach since 1976. Formal divisions, such as monitors placed opposite each other, or clearly demarcated images correspond to themes like the North-South conflict or the relationship between the past and the present. This is the area of conflict which also concerns *As if Memories Could Deceive Me*. In playing Schumann's composition "Manfred" at the piano, Odenbach demonstrates one element of his own cultural identity: the careful upbringing of Germany's educated middle-class children. Suddenly, a drumming sound interrupts and destroys the pretence of harmony. Added to this, the monitors show contrasting images of locally-found objects. When Odenbach showed this work for the first time in Boston in 1986, he found the black garbage bags used there suitable for making the point of his theme.   *D.S.*

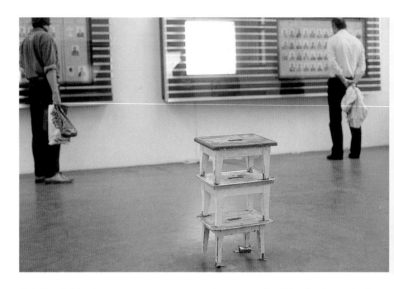

Reinhard Mucha   born 1950
lives in Düsseldorf

Dokumente I–IV   1992
Dokument I / Goslar
Dokument II / Lehrte
Dokument III / Oppeln
Dokument IV / Stryck
Dokument Greven
(additional document)

1 sculpture, 4 wall objects
each 4 $^1/_2$ ft. x 11 ft. x 10 $^1/_2$ in.

Nationalgalerie, acquired 1996 with proceeds from
the German Lottery, Berlin

The installation *Dokumente I–IV*
consists of four wall objects that are
mounted like display cabinets on
four opposite walls. In the middle of
the room are three footstools placed
one on top of the other. Reinhard
Mucha developed this environment
for the documenta 9 in Kassel. The
title of the work refers to this.

The cabinets are divided up horizontally by aluminium bands that are
set into the wall surface. The main
part of the cabinets is covered with
gray woolen felt. At the front, a
square electric light is built in on the
left side and a display board is on the
right. They are protected by two
sliding glass doors of differing sizes.
Their backs have been painted with
lines in three colors (brown, dark

brown, and red lead). The main focus
of the wall objects is on groups of
photographs produced in 1975 for
the works council elections of the
Rheinstahl Foundry AG in Gussstahl-
werk, Oberkassel. Photographs and
names of the candidates from the
metal workers' union IG-Metall are
mounted on pieces of light blue
hardboard. Three similar such photo
boards are exhibited which once
hung in different sections of the foundry. The board in the fourth display
cabinet is empty of photos. Its display area is covered with gray felt.

Reinhard Mucha's work deals with
the rules of visual communication
and the reception of art. The installation with the pictures of the employ-
ees is in that respect ideal as the
function of the images has been
removed from a company and transferred to a museum. The change in
the setting means that the images are
no longer automatically received in a
certain way. These photographs,
which were once familiar and taken
for granted, now become disconcert-
ing artefacts.

Mucha's display cabinets exhibit
the works council photos like reli-
quaries, translating the images into
another visual idiom. The electrically
shining white square might be a play

on Kasimir Malewitsch's *Black Square* and the demise of representational art. However, more interesting than these references to intrinsically artistic matters are the setting and context in which the work is placed. The installation *Dokumente I–IV* has been elevated to museum art. The basic requirements for museum presentation become the theme: framing and lighting, pedestals and glass cabinets used for storing and presenting pictures and sculptures.

The three stacked stools in the middle of the room represent a place to linger. The fact that they are taken from a worker's or lower-class household and are stacked in a makeshift manner to the height of a proper bench (symbolic of an elitist appreciation of art), refers to the museum as a middle-class institution. The fragile and tragi-comical character of this small "architecture" is emphasized by the measuring tape lying on the floor under one of the legs of the stool. Was it supposed to determine the center of the room or the height of the stools, or was it really part of the now lopsided construction? "The medium is the message." With this sentence, Marshall McLuhan describes the theoretical context of

Mucha's conceptual art. It means that communication, be it visual or lingual, achieves one thing above all, and that is to give information about itself. *I.W.D.*

Rolf Julius   born 1939
lives in Berlin

4 floor constructions:
4-part sound sculpture   1994

Measurements vary according to
construction

Nationalgalerie, acquired 1994 with aid from the
Artists' Sponsorship Fund of the Senate's Office for
Science, Research, and Culture, Fine Arts Department,
Berlin

The works of Rolf Julius probe the
border between visual art and music.
They belong to the traditions of the
minimalist music of John Cage. It is
not the visual expression, but rather
the awareness of space and the self
created by sound which are the
prime concerns of his concept. He
consciously avoids an arrangement
of technical equipment. The iron
plate, the loudspeakers in small
bowls of water, the CD-player and
cables are only incidentally noticed.
The soft sounds and noises overlap-
ping each other allow our percep-
tions to float and merge.

   "I have been concerned for a long
time with the question of how to
make spaces in which one can with-
draw, in which one can find peace
and quiet, … in which one can be
shut off from the outside world yet
still take part in it. I am thinking
about … spaces, also perhaps without windows, spaces with just one

piece of work, a suspended iron
plate for example, which appears
to float with the music"
(R. Julius 1987).   *I. W. D.*

Christina Kubisch   born 1948
lives in Berlin

The True and the False   1992
32 $^3/_4$ x 13 ft.

Nationalgalerie, acquired 1992 with aid from the
Artists' Sponsorship Fund of the Senate's Office for
Science, Research, and Culture, Fine Arts Department,
Berlin

The True and the False — the title of
this work has a programmatic character. Loudspeakers with cables are
mounted on a wall. If the speakers
were moved into a horizontal plane,
they might look like waterlilies. The
cables and the covers over the mem-
branes have a plant-like structure.
White pigment lies like pollen on the
circular covers. Even the tones of the
sound installation evoke natural
noises. They are the delicate tones
produced by glasses that have been
set vibrating. The room in which the
installation is contained has been
flooded with black light (ultraviolet
light). The viewer experiences this
light, which approaches the furthest
borders of human perception, perhaps as moonlight.

We see a demonstration of how fragmentary our perception is. Light and sound have the ability to counteract the material character of the technical elements. The insecurity in sudden darkness, without knowledge and recognition, creates space for new experiences. Christina Kubisch applies the theory of the sublime, once applied to the emphatic experience of nature by Edmund Burke, to the border between nature and technology. The true and the false are neither explained nor defined; they are merely passed on to the viewer as a problem of recognition.   *I.W.D.*

Jakob Mattner   born 1946
lives in Berlin

Zwielicht (Twilight)   1992
Glass, light source
Maximum height 9 $^3/_4$ ft.

Nationalgalerie, acquired 1995 with aid from the Artist's Sponsorship Fund of the Senate's Office for Science, Research, and Culture, Fine Arts Department, Berlin

In the works of Jakob Mattner, shadows take on concrete and complex forms. They are the actual sculpture. Through constructivist precision and clarity of plastic shaping, the controlled play of light and shade results in an ephemeral imitation of seeing. Absorbing the concepts of the Russian avant-garde, Mattner chooses simplicity of sculptural means for his designs on the wall. The shadows, the immateriality, the illusion of the image, the variety of forms created by contrasts of darkness and light force the viewer to ask: what is real, what is illusion, what is the picture?
     B.S.

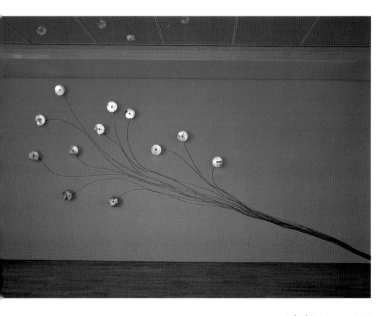

Raffael Rheinsberg born 1943
lives in Berlin

Documenta der Kleinplastiken
(documenta of Small Sculptures)
1987–93

297 objects   65 $^3/_4$ x 49 $^1/_4$ ft.
(entire area)

Nationalgalerie, acquired 1994 with aid from the
Artists' Sponsorship Fund of the Senate's Office for
Science, Research, and Culture, Fine Arts Department,
Berlin

Raffael Rheinsberg throws the viewer
into a cosmos of marginalia. 297
small parts of milling machines and
lathes for metalwork, arranged over a
surface of approximately 65 by 49
feet, make up his *Documenta der
Kleinplastiken*. Objects of unconscious beauty are brought together in
a severely geometric order. Even the
smallest bit of metal forms a vital part
of the whole.

None of these objects used by
Rheinsberg were made by him. They
have all been taken out of their context: they are rubbish, rejects, defec-
tive parts, unusable material. By
treating this degraded material so
protectively, Rheinsberg shows him-

self to be not only an artist, but a
philosopher and social critic as well.

The words of Maguerite Duras,
that forgetting is the real remember-
ing, describe the aesthetic direction
Raffael Rheinsberg is following. The
artist seeks the imprint of our society
at the places where it discards and
divides the useless from the useful.

I.W.D.

Hubert Kiecol born 1950
lives in Cologne

25 Treppen (25 Steps)   1990

Concrete   each 13 x 9 $^3/_4$ x 13 in.

Nationalgalerie, acquired 1991 with aid from the
Renée Sintenis Foundation

Hubert Kiecol's sculptures are
remarkable for their small scale.
Their geometrical shapes, their material, concrete, and, not least, their
presentation in space create the
impression of something that has
been left over or forgotten. No child's
game or miniature world is evoked,
but something rather incomprehensible, perhaps even terrible. This
effect is partly achieved by the geo-

abstraction. These forms could be interpreted as something that has been melted down, the incomprehensible remains of a catastrophe.

Kiecol mostly places his works on the floor. Within the rooms in which they are displayed, they fuse together into an ensemble. In this way they separate themselves from their surroundings, which underlines their monolithic character. By avoiding the use of pedestals, the artist removes all traces of pathos and undermines the usual way of viewing art — that is, looking up from below. With some truth, the compact, small sculptures have been called "stumbling blocks," a term which could be perfectly well applied in a deeper sense, too. The twenty-five steps stand in space without any recognizable order; they do not relate to each other, but each stands for itself as a repetition of continually new starts and ascents. This is only discernible from the privileged viewer's extremely high point of view.   I.W.D.

metic, hard forms and the rough, unfinished, and cold concrete. Sometimes the forms are compact houses with windows cut into them and gable roofs; at other times, as in the case of *25 Treppen*, they are only pieces of architecture on the verge of

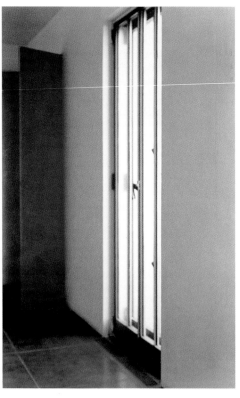

proportion and functional simplicity have become a theme. Unlike in some of his other kinds of work, here, Förg for the most part avoided adopting and tranforming the romantic motif of the view through a window, which for him is never a view into the distance but one often directed at something opposite. The walls of the real exhibition room, its light and its shadows, and the massive frame around the large, coarse-grained photograph break the illusion of other interiors. It is not the view to the outside but the penetration of the outside world into the viewer's space which is the illusion here. The viewer, moreover, is reflected in the glass in front of the photographs.

Günther Förg   born 1953
lives in Areuse

Villa Wittgenstein   1986
Color photo   6 x 4 ft.
The Marx Collection

Günther Förg has applied himself equally to the disciplines of photography, printing, drawing, assemblage and Object Art, panel painting, wall painting, and sculpture in bronze.

Förg's photographs of windows, flights of stairs, or doors in historical architecture follow the concept of sensory "documentation." They relate architectural dimensions and functions to the spatial experience of the individual; they illustrate them or question them. In the exhibition, these photographs give the impression of being separate, fictitious rooms. In the series of photographs taken inside the villa built by Ludwig Wittgenstein in Vienna between 1926 and 1928, stately severity of

His image is integrated into images of historical decoration. Now he himself defines the spirit of the setting in an aesthetic relationship to the photographed architecture. *J.M.*

Gerhard Merz born 1947
lives in Berlin

ED IO ANCHE SON ARCHITETTO
(And I Also Am an Architect) 1988
Pigment on canvas 10 1/2 x 17 1/2 ft.
The Marx Collection

Gerhard Merz wants to create a beauty that breaks down the autonomy of the individual image. Color should appear as a material in its own right. This severe, minimalist approach is relativized by formal classicism and the combination of image and writing. The painter conceives his exhibitions mainly as the shaping of space through color. Color, size, light, and the proportion of the room become means to increase the effect of individual pictures and to develop an intercourse between the colored panels. The architecture of the exhibition room itself is altered in such a way that it integrates the thickly-painted monochrome of the canvas into an order determined by harmony and counterpoint. Consequently, the artist's message, "and I also am an architect" in his painting dated 1988, may be read as a declaration and a programmatic description of himself. Formal severity alongside a decorative quality make the reception of the individual picture problematic, "not so much in the sense of what can be seen, but much more because, 'that is supposed to be all that there is'" (L. Rinn, 1978). Further irritation is caused by the tension between the autonomy of color in the painting and the words in the picture, which break with the picture's meaning by bearing a statement outside the medium of "picture." Photographs, seemingly banal statements, or quotations from world literature are to be found in many works, which trigger historical associations or pose ethical questions. Intellectuality and form are perceived as two sides of one thing: a beauty that can provoke.
J.M.

Schlachtfeld Deutschland

Katharina Sieverding born 1944
lives in Düsseldorf

Schlachtfeld Deutschland XI   1978
(Battlefield Germany XI)

Color photo, acrylic, wood, steel
9 ³/₄ x 12 ¹/₄ ft.

Nationalgalerie, acquired 1993 with aid from the
Artists' Sponsorship Fund of the Senate's Office for
Science, Research, and Culture, Fine Arts Department,
Berlin

Katharina Sieverding employs many
creative techniques in the production
of her large-scale photographs. The
material used is sometimes systemat-
ically chosen or found quite accidentally in newspapers or film stills. The
artist then superimposes images,
accentuates, contrasts, puts photos
deliberately out of focus, manipu-
lates colors to heighten their effect.
The primary impact of her works is
made by the content. Color, structure, and format are the language
of an idea stemming from a serious
involvement in politics. *Schlachtfeld
Deutschland* was exhibited in conjunction with the work group "Kontinentalkern" (Heart of the Continent)
which leans, in a certain sense, on
the Eurasian thoughts of Beuys and
picks up historical as well as more

current themes. These include civilization in East and West, atomic
power and the threat of atomic
destruction, Hiroshima 1945, industrialization and overpopulation, war
in the media, and the Cultural Revolution in China. "Kontinentalkern"
shows documentary photographs,
famous around the world, alongside
unknown pictures: the historically
significant juxtaposed with anony-
mous tragedy.

Schlachtfeld Deutschland shows
only a front: uniformed figures being
trained how to shoot. The emergency
situation is being rehearsed. The darkened scene appears as if seen through
an infrared device. The viewer's position is not threatened. The figures are
facing an imaginary foe. Sieverding
has dispensed with the individuality
of the faces. The inherent formation
of the practice session with its line-up
of figures is similar to the principle of
the series and demonstrates the anonymity of the individual within a
group. Katharina Sieverding asks
questions about the many forms of
latent and real danger to man from
which no social system, no culture,
no industry is free.   *J.M.*

Michael Schmidt born 1945

lives in Berlin

Waffenruhe (Cease-Fire)   1985–87

Photographic series in 9 parts
5 x 4 ft. (complete measurement)

Nationalgalerie, acquired 1992 with aid from the Artists' Sponsorship Fund of the Senate's Office for Science, Research, and Culture, Fine Arts Department, Berlin

Berlin is subject matter and inspiration for the extensive photographic work of Michael Schmidt. One of his series, made up of many parts, is called "Waffenruhe." It is not difficult to apply the title to its historical setting, the divided city. Deserted streets, derelict yards, the repeated motif of the Wall that divided the city, empty plots of land undeveloped since the war, meagre vegetation amidst the ruins of urban life, close-up details of all of these things, and portraits. The hand, with the scar on its wrist is also a portrait. These are images of the injured soul of mankind in the midst of a hopeless history turned to stone and iron, and its hopeless rudiments. The motifs are unremarkable and yet shocking in the uncompromising way they bring to light the banality and violence of everyday life, the environment of the people in this city.   *J.M.*

Thomas Ruff   born 1958
lives in Düsseldorf

Portrait of Elke Denda   1988
C-print   5 $^1/_4$ x 4 ft.

Nationalgalerie, acquired 1993 with proceeds from
the German Lottery, Berlin

Thomas Ruff   born 1958
lives in Düsseldorf

Portrait of Lukas Duwenhögger
1986
C-print   5 $^3/_4$ x 4 $^1/_2$ ft.

Nationalgalerie, acquired 1992 with proceeds from
the German Lottery, Berlin

Since about 1984, Thomas Ruff has been taking large-scale photographic portraits representing people of his own generation. He has produced more than a hundred up to the present day.

How casually they gaze out from the wall, out of the frame into space. Portrayed are his circle of friends and people from the art scene. The young women and men appear immediately familiar, even to strangers. They all seem completely natural, their faces relaxed and expressionless. The realism of the faces fascinates: the almost merciless close-up perspective from which no skin blemish, no stubble can hide. At the same time the pictures have a matter-of-fact, severe, and almost ascetic feeling about them. Their sobriety goes beyond that of all the masses of pictures we are confronted with every day. Strict frontality, a principled and already "serial" conforming and ordering of the figures, plus the avoidance of any expressiveness, are the typical features of the series. The models are bathed in light and are fully exposed to the viewer's gaze. The backgrounds, clothing, and jewelry are chosen by the models themselves.

Surface, line, colors, and structure lend the people portrayed a universal, public dimension comparable to the painted portraits of religious and worldly rulers. Ruff gives us the opportunity to encounter images of people in peace and perfect quiet, without any fashionable distractions. The classic, balanced composition and structure of the entire series evokes thought on the image of mankind as it has been passed down over the centuries.

Along with Thomas Struth, Thomas Ruff attended the Düsseldorf Akademie and the classes of Bernd and Hilla Becher who, likewise, by use of a serial method of working, make the differences between similarities understood.   *B.S.*

Thomas Struth   born 1954
lives in Düsseldorf

San Zaccaria   1995
C-print   6 x 7 $^1/_2$ ft.
The Marx Collection

On looking at the photograph of the interior of the church San Zaccaria in Venice, which Thomas Struth has made the size and format of an Italian masterpiece, the viewer is at once irritated — overpowered by the colossal presence, the vivid colors, and the immediacy of the picture.

The eye is drawn to the center, to the altarpiece by Giovanni Bellini. The columns to the left and right at the edges of the photograph give the dimensions and emphasize the vertical, a movement which is taken up again in the pilasters of the altarpiece. The visitors in the lower third of the photograph increase the sense of scale.

The closeness and depth of the different planes in the picture seem to have been compressed into an inseparable whole. Everything is equally sharp and colorful. Struth has not applied any particular values to his picture; everything has the same significance — the visitors, the architecture, the paintings, and the chairs. There is a type of all-over principle here, just as there is in painting.

The visitors to the church, tourists in casual clothing, sit in the pews and study the high altar with varied degrees of concentration.

The peace exuding from the picture is suited to the setting and to the way Struth works. He always takes a truly characteristic slice of real life and depicts it as part of a strict composition. Struth takes a great deal of care in choosing where to stand for his photographs, and spends a long time in the studio sifting through the material until he finds the right picture.

The public space of the church, set rigidly in its historical and functional context, is transported by the private activities of tourists into the viewer's reality. It becomes the people who move within it, and so the depiction becomes a condensation of personal reality.   *B.S.*

Keith Haring 1958–90

Untitled   1983

Acrylic on vinyl cloth   10 x 10 ft.

The Marx Collection

From December 1980 onwards, in his search of a universally understood visual language, Keith Haring took advantage of the fact that unrented advertising space in the New York subway was pasted over with matt, black rolls of paper. He drew on this using white chalk, something which connects his work with graffiti even though his artistic means were quite contradictory.

While graffiti painters force their way at night into the subway train switching yards and, after precisely planning the design, spray the cars with elaborately stylized and coded signatures, Haring abandoned himself to spontaneous inspiration and drew with an easily erasable material on surfaces that were temporarily free. He worked during the day, discussed his actions with passersby, and dutifully paid his fines.

The subway drawings made Haring so well-known that he was invited to the documenta 7 in Kassel in 1982. His art, influenced by comics, graffiti, and archaic symbols, would seem to show a spiritual affinity to A.R. Penck. The differences, however, are more marked. Penck's theme was divided Germany, he preferred stick figures, his paint was applied in a painterly fashion; Haring, on the other hand — almost twenty years younger — started with drawing, formed figures from contours, and made reference to his multi-cultural environment in the USA.

Haring soon started to paint using brilliant colors on vinyl sheets edged with metal eyelets. On November 6, 1983, he produced the figure of an angular, black machine-like being implanted with a gold chip. At first sight looking rather like a comic figure such as Batman, it stretches out its claw-like arms to kill people and pile them up into a mound of corpses. The cross inside each head symbolizes human existence blotted out. This depiction is programmatic for the artist: "My painting must have something to do with people; it has to put up a defence against technology and our computer-controlled society."

During a stay in Cologne, on May 7, 1984, Haring painted a picture edged in red, showing on the left a break-dancer in gym shoes dancing to the music from a cassette recorder. The ghettoblaster has taken on the form of a skull; the naked woman in the center, who is touching the genitals of a man, is being attacked by a monster who drives stakes through her body. The terrifying, gaping jaws of hell complete the composition in which Haring has confronted the contemporary scene with an apocalyptic motif straight out of the Middle Ages.

What at first seems like a boisterous party

Keith Haring

1958–90

Untitled   1984

Distemper on paper on canvas   5 x 9 ³/₄ ft.

The Marx Collection

reveals itself after closer observation to be a double-edged commentary on the contemporary situation: in the mid 1980s, sexuality again became something to be feared due to the outbreak of the immune-deficiency Aids. The American President, Ronald Reagan, and the Pope dammed homosexuality as unnatural; as one directly affected, Haring went on the offensive. Free sex having always been one of his central themes, he publicized safer sex using posters, stickers, and T-shirts among other things in order to spread his warning. At the same time, he tried as ever to communicate his positive feelings towards the body and joy in confrontation and communication.

The enormous mask (Untitled) from 1987 seems, in hindsight, to be an attempt by Haring to ward off all the evil that beset him with the magic of the pictorial symbols. The artist was continually aware also of the dangers of present-day life. These are obvious only at a second glance; concealed as they are underneath the witty, bright surfaces of his pictures. In the catalogue to the documenta 1982, Haring acknowledged his fears in view of the state of the world: "I am scared to death."   *D. S.*

Keith Haring   1958–90

Untitled   1987
Enamel paint on aluminum
6 1/4 x 4 1/2 x 3/4 ft.
The Marx Collection

Jean-Michel Basquiat   1960–88

Because It Hurts the Lungs   1986
Acrylic, oil, collage on panel
6 x 3 $^1/_2$ x $^3/_4$ ft.
The Marx Collection

Jean-Michel Basquiat was born in Brooklyn, New York in 1960. In his Puerto Rican-born mother and his father, Gerard, who came from a rich Haitian family, a nature-bound power lives on, for whose magic the modern age has developed a distinct sense of longing. Although Basquiat and his graffiti seem to have come out of a sub-cultural underground with all its typical social problems, he in fact grew up in an orderly upper-middle-class environment. Basquiat relinquished his career as a graffiti artist quite early on and began to paint on various moveable surfaces, such as doors or metal sheets. In 1981 in Modena, Italy, he had his first successful solo exhibition and one year later met Andy Warhol. In the following period, the "Collaborations" were produced. These numerous jointly-painted pictures, which were at first badly received by the critics, still permitted each artist to work in his own style.

Basquiat's style cannot be categorized easily. He developed an additive technique in which everything the artist came across was treated equally: heads, airplanes, cars, restaurant menus, and advertisements. The works of art by American modernists belong equally to this list: from Pollock to de Kooning, Rothko and Kline to Warhol, as if they too were everyday objects.

Basquiat fought like one possessed against the omnipotence of facts. They become magical spells in his pictures; banal menus become recipes from a voodoo ritual. Just as Jimi Hendrix had expressed his joy and despair about the reality around him by virtuoso passages on the guitar, Basquiat reacted to American society with a virtuoso "intuitive primitivism." However, he did not know how to cope with its successful marketing and consequential reabsorption into the circulation of "facts." Jean-Michel Basquiat died on August 12, 1988 from a drug overdose.   E.B.

Julian Schnabel   born 1951
lives in New York

He Had a Hat   1983
Oil, modeling paste on carpet
12 x 9 ft.
The Marx Collection

Joseph Beuys was an enormous
source of inspiration for Julian
Schnabel. Europe is an important
area of reference for the artist. It is
here that he seeks the traditions of
painting, knowing full well that it is
difficult to find the new and fresh,
the truly great theme. Schnabel
places himself within this tradition

and fills his pictures with the rem-
nants of many cultures. The materiality of the painting He Had a Hat,
with its red-brown, earthy, nuanced
tonality, is of great importance. The
picture is coarsely textured and contains a sense of depth based on traditional composition. The dominating
feature, along with the archaic man,
is the play between the closed and
the open areas which are encrusted
as they expose yet another underly-
ing layer. These express something
fragmentary that has evolved through
the overlappings of ages and cul-
tures.   *B.S.*

Fiona Rae born 1963
lives in London

Untitled (Gray with Rectangles)
1991

Oil on canvas   7 x 6 ¹/₂ ft.
The Marx Collection

We stand in awe before the paintings of Fiona Rae with their potpourri of different painting styles. They carry a visual language known to us from the computer. Elements that are reduced in size, dismembered, isolated, or distorted by extreme close-up perspectives are the components of a new type of composition. Fiona Rae offers a feast for our eyes with her unhierarchical approach and direct, urban style.

Since 1989, she has not titled her pictures but has numbered them consecutively and identified them according to their main colors. She deliberately places these attributions in brackets, since any associations evoked should only be stimulated visually. Sometimes the application of paint is impasto, then the strokes break off abruptly, showing the artist's masterly control.

Fiona Rae belongs to a younger generation which lets everything fuse together into a universal scheme. The style of painting conforms to incongruous laws: sometimes it serves as a mediator between the viewer and any resulting conclusions, at other times everything submerges into uncertainty, implying that the art can offer no center; no plane is worthy of acceptance. Corresponding features and cross-references to other works are not expressive elements in Rae's work.   B.S.

Peter Halley   born 1953
lives in New York

Zone   1993
Acrylic, metallic acrylic on canvas
6 1/2 x 6 1/4 ft.
The Marx Collection

Both of Halley's paintings in The Marx Collection, *Zone* from 1993 and *History and Memory* from 1994, represent a more recent group of works which, through minimal changes, differ slightly from earlier works. Superficially observed, they still exhibit Halley's basic compositional structure of mostly square fields connected by tubes or linking paths.

In *Zone* there is an isolated red square whose undefined inner life is fed by colored tubes of different sizes which at the same time draw data and energies out of the square. These linking paths lead beyond the edge of the picture to other squares or "cells." We see a tiny detail in an infinite network. In *History and Memory*, the dark tonality is appropriate to the theme. Historical processes and our experience and memory of them seem to be, in our hyper-modern society, just as channeled and meaningless as the incessant transport of data and energies. No meaning is final; the symbols are arranged one behind the other like an endless band, a perpetual circular movement that only keeps itself in motion as a meaningless cycle.   *E.B.*

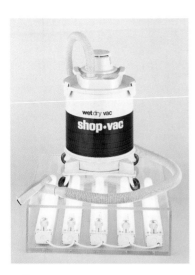

Jeff Koons born 1955
lives in New York

New Shop — Vac Wet/Dry 1980
Vacuum cleaner, plexiglass, tube
lighting 35 x 11 x 22 in.
The Marx Collection

With his art, Jeff Koons takes on the
artificiality of a developed, cultural,
western society, and exposes it in
order to make a general statement.

Koons' conceptual treatment of the
banal, embarrassing, and kitschy
involves the viewer by making him
part of the concept, too.

The objects disguise nothing,
they are not altered to mask their
effect as had previously happened
when ready-made objects entered
the realms of art. Koons' objects are
so insistent in the way they present
themselves that doubts are immediately aroused about the actual
character of the works.

New Shop — Vac Wet/Dry of 1980
is remarkable for its triviality and
utter nakedness. Its pedestal, the
plexiglass, and neon tubes make
the work extremely cold and unap-
proachable, but also decorative and
bright. When it was first exhibited
in the display window of the New
Museum in New York, this manner of
presentation had the expected effect.
Many passersby came into the

museum to ask if they could pur-
chase the vacuum cleaner under the
assumption that they were in a shop
for household appliances.

The apparent similarities to Pop Art
are, in fact, misleading. The artificiality exuding from Jeff Koons' works
does not orient itself on reality and
the experiences of reality, but measures itself, instead, against the inten-
sifying degrees of abstraction in society and art.

The vacuum cleaner drives away
all thoughts of dirt, routine, effort, or
sweat. The machine remains ageless
or eternally young. Koons even
avoided "defiling" it with his finger-
prints. In addition, it is a useless
product, condemned to a cold
standstill, to rigor mortis. Having
relinquished its purpose, it can only
survive as a fetish.

Both the basketballs floating in distilled water in *Two Ball 50/50 Tank*
belong to the "Equilibrium" series in

Jeff Koons born 1955
lives in New York

Bourgeois Bust — Jeff and Ilona
1991
Marble 44 1/2 x 28 x 21 in.
The Marx Collection

which Koons takes real, new balls whose normal function involves a communicative team sport, and alienates them from their intended purpose. The artist wanted to achieve an absolute balance. He wanted to evoke associations with amniotic fluid, the fruits of the womb, and purity. Koons therefore used distilled water, which holds the balls in balance and does not let them sink to the floor of the tank. At some point the balls begin to interact, setting off a pattern of thought in which information is thrown back and forth between them. And yet, like the vacuum cleaner, the balls are also unused, brand new, showing no signs of having been handled. The eternal newness, the ideal of the unused, counteracts at the same time the possibilities of interaction and subtly refers to the phenomenon in American society that basketball is traditionally played among lower-class blacks whose success in the game leads to an improvement of their status in society.

Jeff Koons   born 1955
lives in New York

Two Ball 50/50 Tank   1985
Glass, steel, water, 2 basketballs
62 ³/₄ x 36 ³/₄ x 13 ¹/₄ in.
The Marx Collection

Bourgeois Bust — Jeff and Ilona from 1991 is a portrait of the artist and his girlfriend at that time, Ilona Staller (La Cicciolina). In his work, Koons often makes explicit reference to the extremely artificial use of forms in the Rococo in order to demonstrate artificiality as a generalizing process. The works, which are close to kitsch, are intentionally banal and yet also extremely seductive. La Cic-

ciolina is in this case the covetous one; both figures are pure art who, as artificial, lifeless, and over-exaggerated representations of attraction, love, and sex, demonstrate how our society functions. Koons' passion for an artificial, mannered, and Rococo-like style is connected with the coldness of frozen, reduced, and diminishing feelings.   *B.S.*

Cindy Sherman   born 1954
lives in New York
Untitled # 44 (Film Still)   1979
Black-and-white photo   8 x 10 in.
The Marx Collection

Cindy Sherman grew up bombarded with the clichés produced in Hollywood. In films, stories are told which, due to the realism of their photography and acting, appear very close to reality while at the same time revealing themselves to be a masquerade.

Sherman is searching for the psycho-social phenomena of the twin female existence, which she captures in her photographs in any form from role-plays to specially-constructed horror figures. Transformation is seen as an escape and a cry for help, as awakening and destruction.

Untitled # 44 (Film Still) from 1979 awakens memories of the black-and-white films of the 1950s. What is so unsettling and perhaps even shocking about the "Film Stills" is the merciless reduction of the figure, the stills' narratively logical or illogical, unconditional development towards the moment of perfect disguise.

From the outset, Sherman works towards capturing the essential quality of a figure — which she can only do if she herself is this figure. After the "Fairy Tale-Pictures" came the "History Portraits" (1988–90), large-scale color photographs that attempt to reconstruct the figurative gesture of Old Master paintings. When she shows a Judith in her *Untitled #228 (History Portrait)*, with her blood-smeared knife in one hand and the head of Holofernes in the other, she brutally strips away all the magic of the visual world she is investigating. In fact, the "History Portraits" do not analyze painting, which has merely provided the costumes, but rather the invention of the image. In the ambivalence between falsified paintings and genuine photographs, Sherman questions and comments ironically on a superficial way of experiencing art which is characterized by false pathos.   *E.B.*

Cindy Sherman   born 1954
lives in New York
Untitled #228 (History Portrait) 1990
Color photo   6 ³/₄ x 4 ft.
The Marx Collection

Matthew Barney   born 1967

lives in New York

Cremaster 1: Orchidella   1996

Color photo in plastic frame
43 $^1/_2$ x 53 $^3/_4$ in.

The Marx Collection

In the spirit of gene-technology and virtual reality, Matthew Barney can be considered equally as a belated mannerist or as a prophet of a "post-human" age.

His works of the late 1980s have as themes the world of fitness studios, bodybuilders, and athletes who intentionally deform their bodies in order to achieve extreme goals outside their normal limits of performance. In his video projects of the 1990s, the investigation was shifted from the individual development of the body to a field of collective new inventions. Fairies and satyrs appeared in the pictures as well as spaceship crew members and formation dancers.

The fourth part of the planned five-part video series "Cremaster" was the first one to be produced, filmed on the Isle of Man in 1994.

In the first part, which was realized in 1995, revue girls in an American stadium circle a central figure in whose image they seem to have been modeled. In another scene, the same person becomes a distant deity inside an airship hovering above the playing field. The pattern she makes from grapes is copied by the dancers on the ground. Barney makes a travesty of the heavenly creation — he calls it a "biological farce" — by using stylistic elements from dance revues of the 1940s sprinkled with a few science fiction motifs, and arrives at a new mythology whose holy solemnity is dissolved playfully in the medium of dance.

According to its Greek origins, "Cremaster" is that which holds things high. Anatomically, this refers to the muscle that contracts to regulate the temperature of the testicles. At the same time, "cré" is the shortened form of "sacré." "Cremaster" is thus the holy master or the holy championship.   *D.S.*

Rebecca Horn   born 1944
lives in Bad König and Berlin

Raum des verwundeten Affen   1990
(Room of the Wounded Monkey)

1 paper cutter, 1 telescope, 2 metronomes, 3 sets of copper coils, metal constructions, motors, electric cable
Measurements vary according to
construction.

Nationalgalerie, acquired 1990 by the state of Berlin

In 1994, the Nationalgalerie put on a
retrospective exhibition on Rebecca
Horn showing the different facets of
her work. Out of the great hall of the
Mies van der Rohe building, a radiant stream of snaking tubes poured
forth to the city outside. The artist
opened wide the museum's interior
with this run of her *El rio de la luna*,
which had been specially altered for
Berlin. The dramatic character of the
town, her original inspiration twenty
years ago and the place where she
has been working as a professor
since 1989, was in this way allowed
to flow in.

Her body sculptures of the 1970s,
the participation objects in her first
solo exhibition "Körperraum" (Body-
Spaces; Berlin, 1973), and the film
sequences *Berlin-Übungen in neun
Stücken* (Berlin Exercises in Nine
Pieces; 1974–75) translated psycho-
logical situations into spatial happenings set to rhythms. Her films
communicated dramatic conflict
through a tension-filled dialogue
between the moved objects and the
"acting" space. With poetic language, rich in metaphor, Rebecca
Horn gives form to the vicious circle
of erotic desire, permanent aggres-
sion, painful injuries, and unfulfilled
longing for security. The actors are
technically perfected machines. Spe-
cifically chosen technical and chem-
ical materials with mystical associations serve as expressive vehicles for
the unstoppable mechanism of attraction and repulsion. It is out of this
ambivalence of distance and closeness, finiteness and infinity, reason

and emotion, magic and reality that
the surreal expression of her works
grows. Since the second half of the
1980s, both the space and time elements in Rebecca Horn's work have
won a new, historical dimension; she
seeks out settings with dark, incrimi-
nating pasts and intervenes as an irri-
tant in the transformation achieved
by time. In 1986, in the neoclassical
foyer of the Viennese Theater at Stein-
hof, which was integrated into a
psychiatric clinic, she installed a
Schwarzes Bad (Black Bath) with
Pendel (Pendulum) and *Ballett der
Spechte* (Ballet of the Woodpeckers)
for the show "Wien Fluss" (Vienna
River). For the 1987 exhibition in
Münster called "Skulptur Projekte,"
she produced *Das gegenläufige Kon-
zert* (The Counter-Rotating Concert),
a penetrating installation recalling
Germany's recent past, and situated
in an old prison tower in which the
Gestapo executed prisoners. From
that time on, she has taken history as
her theme by using spaces haunted
by radical events of the past and con-
fronting them with the present.

When the Wall came down in Berlin, along with the dramatist, Heiner
Müller, and the artist, Jannis Kounellis, she realized the idea, conceived
four years previously, of a joint installation which was now to comment
on the changed political situation.
Under the title formulated by Heiner
Müller "Die Endlichkeit der Freiheit"
(The Finiteness of Freedom), eleven
international artists were each able
to develop a work in a setting of their
choice in the eastern or western half
of the divided city which formed a
dialogue with the opposite half. Rebecca Horn, however, concentrated
on a setting in the no man's land
between east and west. She discovered a bricked-up shop at Strese-
mann Straße 128 directly on the
border, full of dusty files and a
paper-cutting machine from the
1920s. This was where she installed
her *Raum des verwundeten Affen*.
The knife of the cutting machine,

which bears a resemblance to the head of a monkey and inspired the artist to choose a title based on the story by the brothers Grimm, cuts the air we breathe. Two metronomes at the sides beat out of synchronization with each other in the differing times of east and west. Built into the wall, an oversized pair of binoculars stares at the Wall, behind which lies the *Fluß der Angst zu ertrinken* (River of the Fear of Drowning). Hissing

electric flashes release their explosive energy into the gloom from the copper coils on the ceiling. By placing the installation in such a claustrophobic room, Rebecca Horn expresses the electric atmosphere of the city which had been divided for decades, a city tense with confrontation and alienation, threats and violence, division and imprisonment.

F.W.

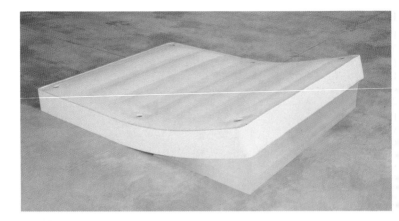

Rachel Whiteread   born 1963
lives in London
Untitled   1991
Rubber, foam rubber   15 x 76 x 60 in.
The Marx Collection

object, which is also representative
of an individual history has, at the
same time, a social, public level of
meaning.   *B.S.*

The "familiar strangeness" of
Whiteread's sculptures is caused
by their associations and memories
which touch our immediate surroundings. These associations are,
however, not specific enough to be
linked to the history of one particular
individual. On the contrary, they remain generalized. Each individual

Rachel Whiteread   born 1963
lives in London
Study for Wax Floor   1992
Correcting fluid, ink on graph paper
18 x 12 in.
Kupferstichkabinett, acquired 1996 with aid from the
Artists' Sponsorship Fund of the senate's Office for
Science, Research, and Culture, with proceeds from
the German Lottery, Berlin

Similar to her sculptures, Whiteread's
works on paper also bear a relationship to the material elements of
everyday experience. This connection is clear from the motif but is relativized with the help of the form it
takes. The floor plans in her gou-
aches relate to her casts taken from
wall partitions or mobile scenery.
Her drawing reproduces the floor
boards of the corridor as viewed
from above; because of this perspective and her dividing of the portrayed
area into three parts, her image is
reduced to an almost abstract form.
While the sculptures have a graphic
quality due to their surface structure,
the works on paper possess a haptic
quality expressed in the impasto
application of the correcting fluid
which defines the contours of the
floor boards.   *A.D.*

Piotr Nathan   born 1956

Puppenkleiderschneider
1986–88
(Tailor of Dolls' Clothes)
Dress (1988): fabric, pine
cones   19 3/4 x 47 1/4 x
39 1/4 in.

Paintings (1986): oil on canvas, collected items painted
over, threads, iron hooks
each 23 1/2 x 31 1/2 in.

Nationalgalerie, acquired 1996 with
aid from the Artists' Sponsorship Fund
of the senate's Office for Science, Research, and Culture, with proceeds from
the German Lottery, Berlin

The title of the sculpture
Puppenkleiderschneider,
which hangs from many fine threads,
evokes memories of childhood. The
blue dress, its fabric covered with
pine cones, is situated in a moment
of peace, in a state of suspension.
This happy moment can at any time
be set in motion, the balance destroyed. Such instability, a theme
throughout the works of the Polish
exile Piotr Nathan, stimulates questions about the fragile and insecure
state of our world at the end of the
20th century.   *B.S.*

Maria Eichhorn   born 1962
lives in Berlin

Vorhang (grau); (Curtain, gray) Six
texts by Margarita Albrecht, Marius
Babias, Knut Bayer, Gerti
Fietzek, Heinz-Werner
Lawo, Reiner Matzker
1990–91
Museum information stand
made out of plexiglass
37 1/2 x 9 3/4 in.

Gray curtain
Measurements vary accor-
ding to construction

Nationalgalerie, acquired 1991 with
aid from the Artists' Sponsorship Fund
of the senate's Office for Cultural Affairs, Berlin

On a typical museum
information stand are
sheets of paper which can
be removed. On them, six people
describe how they managed to solve
a task set by the artist: by connecting
different small letters of a type grid,
they formed the word-picture *AL-
PHABET*. The linguistic representation of an action becomes a presentation in the installation, as the
curtain gives the impression that
there is a stage hiding behind it.
What is concealed behind the
curtain is, in fact, a blank wall. The
debate on the classic problem of
art, the feigning of reality — also a
theme in Gerhard Richter's painting
Vorhang (Curtain) — is continued
in Maria Eichhorn's play on the
construction and deconstruction of
image and meaning.   *D.S.*

Raimund Kummer   born 1954
lives in Berlin

Mehr Licht (More Light)   1991
Glass, light source

Measurements vary according to construction

Nationalgalerie, acquired 1995 with aid from the Artists' Sponsorship by the senate's Office for Science, Research, and Culture, Fine Arts Department, Berlin, with proceeds from the German Lottery

At first sight, Raimund Kummer's floor work has the appearance of a glass-bead game. Looking more closely, we notice, however, that bowl-like forms and spheres are not abstract objects. The form of the human eye, with iris and pupil, is the starting point for the glass sculptures. Placed among them are twelve glass plates which are engraved with diagrams. Together, the elements result in a schematic representation of a disturbance of the blood circulation which can lead to blindness. The possible loss of eyesight is not a source of anxiety for the artist alone, but would be critical for his work, for which the optic organ is the most important tool. The German word for "eyesight" ("Augenlicht" — light of

the eye) recalls the ancient concept which considered the eye to be an active transmitter of light. Deprived of its mystique by the mechanistic view of the world, the eye has been known since Descartes to be a passive recording apparatus. Kummer attempts to bring light back into the eyes by shining a strong artificial light onto their arrangement on the black floor. The title Mehr Licht describes the technical concept but at the same time refers to Goethe's last cry from his deathbed, and can thus also be interpreted as a demand for enlightenment.

The metaphor of the eye can be found in much of Kummer's work. For an exhibition in the Brooklyn Museum in 1987, he first bought a glass eye which provided the basis for the trilogy "Corpus Vitreum," whose first part was formed by Mehr Licht. The process of seeing, which has been a theme for Kummer since 1978 — also in the framework of the Büro Berlin, which he co-founded — has been translated into sculptural form: "that which sees, should now also be seen" (R. Kummer).   D.S.

Anish Kapoor   born 1954
lives in London

1000 Names   1980–84
Wood, gesso, pigment
5 pieces   Various measurements
The Marx Collection

1000 Names belongs to a large and important work complex which Anish Kapoor developed over many years.

The group consists of numerous sculptural forms which have been dusted with pure pigments in a few monochrome colors. The forms stand on the floor and are reminiscent of pyramids, volcanoes, mountains, cones, and pedestals. Essentially, it is negative and positive forms which define the respective shapes. The works are connected to the floor on which they stand, since the pigment forms a contour around the shape on the floor. The elements of light and dark, the contradictory and the complementary are fused in these works. Bipolarity characterizes Kapoor's entire artistic concept.

Anish Kapoor, born in India, received his artistic education in England. After a visit to his Indian homeland (1979), he recognized how much his work was influenced by that country. The foreignness of his own culture and the great diversity in the fine arts, both of which he had inherited, have led to his discovery of colors in their purest form and greatest intensity. The pigment dust covering the object creates distance and lends the object a sense of suspension, an aura.

1000 Names is a work of great beauty. Tantric thought seeks beauty in art and its deepest layers of meaning: self-knowledge and knowledge of the world, examination of microcosms and macrocosms.

Along with the captivating clarity and simplicity of the forms, which attain considerable significance in the further development of Kapoor's work, it is the use of pure color which adds to the concentration and impact of his art.

The monochrome complexes make reference to one another and intensify their interwoven relationships when viewed as a whole. Concave or hollowed-out forms already appear in this early work, forms which would be developed further in the especially pronounced depressions and empty spaces of his work in stone. They are not to be perceived as having something missing, but rather should offer space for ideas and imagination.   *B.S.*

142 Günther Uecker

Index of Artists' names

© of illustrated works by the artists, their heirs and assigns, except for works by: Jean-Michel Basquiat, Joseph Beuys, Michael Buthe, Sandro Chia, Enzo Cucchi, Maria Eichhorn, Rainer Fetting, Dan Flavin, Karl Horst Hödicke, Rebecca Horn, Donald Judd, Joseph Kosuth, Raimund Kummer, Roy Lichtenstein, Robert Morris, Bruce Nauman, Blinky Palermo, Robert Rauschenberg, Raffael Rheinsberg, Ulrike Rosenbach, Thomas Ruff, Reiner Ruthenbeck, Wolf Vostell, Franz Erhard Walther by VG Bild-Kunst, Bonn 1997; Andy Warhol by The Andy Warhol Foundation for the Visual Arts / VG Bild-Kunst, Bonn 1997; Georg Baselitz by Georg Baselitz, Derneburg; Jeff Koons by Jeff Koons, New York; Arnulf Rainer by Arnulf Rainer, Vienna 1997.

Library of Congress Cataloging-in-Publication Data
Hamburger Bahnhof. English
  Hamburg Bahnhof, Museum for the Present—Berlin / [translated from the German by Penelope Crowe].
     p. cm. — (Prestel museum guide)
  ISBN 3-7913-1731-8 (English ed.). — ISBN 3-7913-1713-X (German ed.)
  1. Hamburg Bahnhof—Museum for the Present (Berlin, Germany)—Guide books. I. Title. II. Series.
N6488.G3B38795 1997   97-191
708.31′55—dc21   CIP